Herbs!

Creative Herb Garden Themes and Projects

Judy Lowe

Published by Cool Springs Press
P. O. Box 2828
Brentwood, Tennessee 37204

Lowe, Judy.
  Herbs! : creative herb garden themes and projects / Judy Lowe.
      p. cm.
  Includes index.
  ISBN 978-1-59186-490-5 (pbk.)
  1. Herb gardens. 2. Herb gardening. I. Title. II. Title: Dig, plant, grow! Herbs.
III. Title: Baker's dozen herb garden projects.

  SB351.H5L69 2011
  635'.7--dc22

                              2010034940

First Printing 2011
Printed in the United States of America
10 9 8 7

Managing Editor: Billie Brownell, Cover to Cover Editorial Services
Art Director: Sheri Ferguson, Ferguson Design Studio

Herbs!

Creative Herb Garden Themes and Projects

Judy Lowe

COOL SPRINGS PRESS

Growing Successful Gardeners™

www.coolspringspress.com

BRENTWOOD, TEN

Dedication

To David and Randy. No one could ask for two better brothers.

Acknowledgements

As always, this book owes its readability to Billie Brownell, one of the best—and nicest—editors in the business. And it owes its existence to Roger Waynick, a publisher who's always exploring new possibilities. A thousand thank-yous to Cindy Games, who seems to do everything and always does it well. Big thanks also to Elayne Sears for her charming and creative illustrations, to Sheri Ferguson for her great design, and to Jennifer Greenstein, for careful and conscientious copyediting.

I also owe a debt of gratitude to my husband, who never complained once about the moving cartons that didn't get unpacked while I was finishing this project as we moved from Massachusetts to South Carolina. Without these angels in disguise, this book wouldn't be. I'm grateful to them all.

—Judy

Why are herbs so popular? Because they strike the perfect balance between practicality and pleasure. They produce flowers, have varied and interesting fragrances and textures, and are useful in many ways, from cooking to landscaping. Just as nice from a gardener's perspective is that herbs aren't at all difficult to grow. Even beginners can be successful with a wide range of herbs. Many hesitate to try, though, because herbs are such a diverse group of plants that it isn't as easy to know how to grow them as it is, say, a flat of marigolds.

The spelling and pronunciation of the word *herb* have varied down through the ages. In English, the word began as *herb*, with the *h* pronounced. Later, the *h* was dropped in the pronunciation and the word even began to be spelled *erb*. In the Middle Ages, the *h* returned to the spelling, but not to the pronunciation. During the nineteenth century, the British returned the *h* to the pronunciation, too, speaking the word as their American cousins pronounce the man's name. Americans continued with the "old" pronunciation, *urb*. The French, whose word is *herbe*, also pronounce it with a silent *h*.

Introduction

Herbs come in many sizes, from tiny soil-hugging ground covers to shrubs and trees. Some are perennials and return year after year; others are annuals that vanish with the first fall frost.

Still, it's this variety that makes herbs so appealing. An herb garden isn't just green. It can sometimes be a riot of color—bold purple, gold, silver, and bicolor cream-and-green leaves abound in the herb world, joined by flowers in all hues of the rainbow. Fragrances run the gamut from sharp and spicy to sweet and fruity and everything in between.

Kids, as well as adults, enjoy the feast for the senses offered by herbs, caressing the soft, fuzzy leaves of lamb's ears and snapping off a chocolate mint leaf to sniff.

This isn't anything new, of course. Herbs are mentioned frequently in the Bible and in the writings of Shakespeare. They have a long and fascinating history that stretches back to earliest recorded history. We don't know exactly how people began using herbs, but ancient burial sites have included medicinal herbs, and early writings of the Chinese, Egyptians, Romans, and Greeks tell of the study and use of hundreds of herbs to cure ailments of all types.

Herbs Are Useful Plants

Today, the effectiveness of some herbal folk remedies has been disproved. But many modern medicines include plant-derived ingredients or are based on a compound derived from plants.

We may consider ourselves far removed from the ancient Romans or Egyptians, but we use herbs in many of the same ways—for wreaths, cooking, teas and other beverages, bath and cosmetic preparations, flavoring, air freshening, seasoning, and a multitude of other uses.

What is an herb? Many consider it to be any useful plant. You may know some of the plants in this book, such as yarrow and bergamot (bee balm), as perennial flowers, and you may consider others, such as garlic and chives, to be vegetables. But they've all been part of the herb world for hundreds of years.

Designing an Herb Garden

Although this book gives a number of suggestions for creating herb gardens on specific themes and presents illustrations of one way to plant each garden, it does not offer specific plant-by-number designs. This was done deliberately so that you can create gardens that work for your yard and its conditions, and in the spaces you have available.

All too often, gardeners discover generic designs are either too large or too small for their yard, contain plants or colors that the gardener doesn't want to use, and call for plants that are better suited for a warmer or colder climate or for a shady garden when the gardener has full sun, and so on.

We provide lists of herbs that fit the theme of each garden, and then we give you information that helps you decide if they fit into your particular landscape. Do the suggested herbs need moist or dry soil? Are they annual or perennial? How tall will they grow? Can they be grown in small spaces or containers?

The first consideration is to match the herbs you're interested in growing with the conditions you have. More than almost anything else you do, this will determine your success or failure. Ask yourself:

- Do you have sun or shade? Most herbs like full sun, except in the hottest climates, but many will manage just fine in partial shade (about 5 hours of sun each day).

- Does your soil hold moisture well after rain or watering, or does it drain quickly and rapidly dry out? Many herbs, native to the hillsides of the Mediterranean region, are tolerant of dry soil, which is good news for gardeners. But whichever kind of soil you have, grow plants that prefer it. Both kinds of soil can be improved—so moist soil drains better and dry soil holds moisture better—by the addition of organic matter such as compost or rotted leaves.

Other Design Considerations

- Determine the mature height of the herbs you want to grow. While tall plants in back and short ones in front isn't a rigid rule, it works well most of the time when an herb bed has a backdrop (a fence, a house, a tall hedge). But when a bed is an island, or freestanding, taller plants should go in the center of the bed, with the medium ones surrounding them, and the shorter ones on the outside. (The same is true when planting a container.) Exceptions to the rules are where tall, airy plants can go near the front of the bed because they can be seen through, and in cottage gardens, where a group of tall plants may occasionally be placed in the middle.

- Choose pleasing color combinations, not just of flowers but of foliage too.

- Don't overlook the contribution of foliage to garden design. Foliage adds color and texture to the garden. It might be pale green and ethereal or large, solid, and dark green. Grow a variety of plants for best effect.

- A plant's form or habit also matters; does the plant grow upright, in a mound, as a round bush? You can group plants with similar form together or experiment with mixing them to see what interesting effects you can create.

- Create continuity by repeating various colors, textures, and plants in different parts of the garden.

- Formal or informal? Straight lines and equal spacing of plants indicate a formal design. An informal design uses curved lines and some plants spaced closer together and others farther away. An informal design also includes groups and drifts of plants. Make curves smooth and sweeping, not wavy, since too many "waves" are harder to care for. Symmetry—such as planting the same plants on each side of an entrance to a garden—is important in formal gardens.

- A short evergreen hedge or a border of one type of plant will give a sense of unity to an herb garden.

- Don't overlook the value of a focal point, something that catches the eye. This can be an impressive plant or a piece of garden art such as a gazing ball, a statue, or a decorative bird bath.

- What does your house look like? What does your yard look like? Create a garden that's in harmony with the style and appearance of both, not too big or overwhelming. It should fit into its surroundings.

Practical Details

You don't need an entire garden plot for herbs. Search out small, unused spots in your landscape along walkways, islands, against a fence, in borders. And don't overlook containers. You can grow an entire year's worth of culinary herbs in pots that fit nicely on small patios or balconies.

Sketch your design on paper first and do lots of moving and erasing. This is a great winter project.

Then, when you think you have a design you like, lay out your design on the ground using a garden hose and leave in place a few days to make sure you like it. A hose is great because it's flexible and will show curves in your design.

If all this sounds overwhelming, don't let it be. Choose the herbs you really like and those you want to know better and follow the rule of putting them in their right place, with the conditions of sunlight and soil they prefer. Then give them the care they need. (See "Herb Garden Favorites" chapter to learn how to care for all the herbs included in this book.) Your success will prepare you to move on to growing more herbs in gardens designed just for them. You'll find additional ideas on the next pages.

Herbs in the Landscape

Herbs and Ornamentals Make a Good Combination

If you don't have space for a separate herb garden—or even if you do—it's fun to integrate a number of herbs into a flower bed. Start by replacing annual bedding plants such as marigolds and petunias with herbs that have attractive flowers. These include bergamot (bee balm), pot marigold (calendula), some of the salvias (including pineapple sage), tansy, and yarrow.

Herbs with a more subtle floral display integrate well with perennials. Try chives, garlic chives, feverfew, hyssop, lavender, and scented geraniums.

But don't stop with flowers. Silver-leaved herbs are striking when planted with purple sage or bronze fennel. And what perennial border wouldn't be more appealing if edged by a row of dark green curly-leaf parsley or soft, furry lamb's ears?

Herbs Are a Natural With Roses

Lavender and roses aren't just a charming scent combination. They grow well together in the garden, each enhancing the appearance of the other. You'll want to choose easy-care roses as part of an herb garden. Good choices include modern landscape roses and Old Garden roses (those introduced before 1867), which have the romantic appearance you're looking for. They also are extremely fragrant and excellent for potpourri.

Some of these roses bloom only once a year (usually in May to June, depending on where you live) and others flower over and over from spring through fall. Be sure you know which you're getting, so you won't be disappointed.

When there's enough room in the garden, a delightful design is to surround a bed of sweet-smelling herbs with low-growing rosebushes, or vice versa.

Being Stepped On

Most of us try to avoid stepping on plants, but some herbs don't mind being underfoot and even reward those who crush them with a waft of fragrance. Creeping ornamental thymes, such as woolly thyme, are the ideal choice to grow between steppingstones. Chamomile is good too.

Place one plant halfway between each stone in the path and they will spread to fill. Or dig little pockets in a pea gravel walk and tuck variegated lemon thyme into them. It's a happy relationship: the stones keep the soil beneath them cool and moist for the herbs' roots to grow into. Consider planting some herbs, such as lavender or lamb's ears, beside a pathway so that they spill over into the path and soften its lines.

Herbs Cover the Ground

Might your next ground cover be an herb? Several fill the bill nicely—mother-of-thyme, chamomile, mints, creeping rosemary, creeping thyme, violets, and low-growing cultivars of yarrow. And don't overlook sweet woodruff, which forms a nice ground cover in shade and doesn't mind competition from tree roots.

Learn which of those plants are perennial in your climate and which are annual before you plant. Evergreens are most useful, but if you have snow cover in winter, it may not matter.

You will have to weed a new ground cover bed for its first two or three years, but after that, it should suppress weeds on its own.

Herbs Among the Vegetables

Many herbs are already grown in the vegetable garden—dill, garlic, and horseradish among them—so why not plant others together? Basil and tomatoes, for example, like the same growing conditions and are used together in the kitchen. Many herbs appreciate good soil and regular watering, which vegetables automatically receive.

Almost all herbs can be grown in the vegetable garden, but the culinary herbs make themselves particularly at home. These include basil, borage, cilantro/coriander, dill, fennel, garlic, marjoram, sage, summer savory, and thyme.

Herbs That Don't Like Hot, Humid Climates

- *Angelica*
- *Artemisia*
- *Bee balm*
- *Lady's mantle*
- *Lavender*
- *Santolina*
- *Sage*
- *Yarrow*

If you live where heat and humidity are high in summer and want to grow these plants, look for cultivars that are tolerant of your conditions.

The main thing is to separate perennial herbs—chives, fennel, garlic, oregano, sage, and thyme, among them—from the rest of the garden, if it's going to be plowed up annually. Then intersperse the annual herbs with the vegetables.

Herbs on the Edge

Plants chosen to edge an herb garden are typically compact. That's why dwarf boxwood has long been a favorite edging for formal herb gardens. But today's informal gardens have a more natural look, where low-growing cultivars of lamb's ears, lavender, and variegated culinary sage find a happy home as edgers.

Other good choices are chives, curly-leaf parsley, 'Blue Mound' rue, salad burnet, 'Silver Feather' tansy, and creeping thyme.

Herbs Grow Up

Although there aren't any vining herbs that can be trained to grow vertically, you can give ordinary herbs some height by planting them in niches between stones in a wall or in the cracks of a wall that's seen better days. Fill the niches with good soil, place the plant in it, and then firm the soil around its roots.

The best herbs for this purpose will be small with a creeping habit and will not mind the dry conditions—dwarf artemisia, creeping thyme, small rosemary, and ornamental varieties of oregano, for example.

A strawberry jar also gives herbs some height. These containers have great appeal, but are a watering challenge. The key is to buy a piece of PVC pipe and cut it one-quarter inch shorter than the jar. Then hold the pipe in the strawberry jar to measure where the little planting pockets will be located along it. Drill $1/4$-inch holes in the pipe at those points. (For large strawberry jars, you can also use a piece of black drainage pipe used for French drains. It already has holes.)

Have someone help you hold the pipe in place in the jar while you fill the pipe with gravel and then surround the pipe with potting soil to the lower planting pockets. Place a plant in each pocket and add more potting mixture, firming it around the herb's roots. Add more soil and plants to the top. Water the plants through the pipe.

Types of Herb Gardens

Formal Herb Garden

Traditionally, English and European herb gardens were formal and had a geometric shape, with beds neatly edged by low-growing plants and separated by paths of brick, stone, gravel, or mulch. In keeping with their ornamental appearance, formal herb gardens often contain sundials, birdbaths, fountains, statuary, small pools of water, or topiary herbs. They may be surrounded by walls, fences, or hedges and often contain benches or other seating. But because of their simplicity and elegance, they require more maintenance than an informal garden—pruning the plants, sweeping the paths, and making sure the edging is always neat.

Knot Garden

In knot gardens, which became popular in the late fifteenth century, foliage was the focal point. Herbs of varying types, colors, and textures were planted so they grew into intricate designs that mimicked lace or plaster ceiling patterns.

Plan your design on paper first and then trace the design in flour on the ground to see how it will look. The best place for a knot garden is where it can be seen from above.

Because they'll be trimmed frequently during the growing season, the best herbs for a knot garden are woody perennials, including hyssop, germander, lavender, santolina, thyme, and winter savory. Dwarf boxwood is often used too.

Herbs That Are Grown for Their Seeds
- Anise
- Caraway
- Cilantro/Coriander
- Dill
- Fennel

Container Herb Garden

Containers allow gardeners without much land to grow herbs. But potted herbs also provide flexibility, letting plants be grown closer to the kitchen if the herb garden isn't in a convenient location, and letting those with lots of shade to move plants where the sun is.

Containers come in a variety of sizes and textures, which should be matched to the plants you're growing in them. Terra cotta is traditional and lets the herbs be the center of attention, rather than the pot, but doesn't stand up to winter weather. Plastic can be useful, especially in hot climates, since it cuts down on watering slightly. Plastic pots are also available in many sizes and shapes. Don't overlook wood, but make sure the containers aren't made from treated wood, which can leach chemicals. All containers must include drainage holes.

The containers should be tall enough and wide enough to support the herbs' mature height and spread. For herbs that need regular watering, use a good potting mixture, mixed with 1 to 2 cups composted manure as a mild, slow-acting fertilizer. For herbs that like well-drained soil, mix the potting soil with one-third fine bark.

Herbs growing in containers need watering more often than those in the garden. By the end of summer, it's usually daily. All that watering flushes nutrients out the drainage hole, so you'll also want to fertilize herbs in pots more frequently.

Herbs That Tolerate Damp Soil

Bergamot

Comfrey

Mint

Parsley

Herbs in Raised Beds

If your soil is poor or doesn't drain well, a raised bed is a good solution. It also doesn't require any heavy digging. Usually, raised beds are made from wood, but they may also be made from stones or blocks. Whatever the type, the edges need support. The best height is 1 to 2 feet.

Fill the raised bed with good-quality topsoil—combined with up to one-fourth compost and a little composted manure, if available—and water thoroughly. Let the soil settle overnight and add more soil as needed. Rake smooth and water again. Then you're ready to plant.

Warning: Some herbs grow like weeds!

A few herbs can become invasive in your garden, either because they scatter their seeds far and wide or because their roots or rhizomes seem intent on digging for China.

In small gardens, it's best to avoid these bullies altogether or grow them in containers. But sometimes these potential pests are useful for gardeners who have a spot where they can allow a weedy plant to roam—a barren hillside, for instance, or an area where little else will grow.

Why are potentially invasive herbs included in this book? Because not every plant marked as "may be invasive" is invasive everywhere. It may be problematic on the West Coast and okay in the Northeast, or vice versa. I've grown yarrow in several different climates without any problems at all, yet I've had gardening friends who rue the day they planted it.

The second reason that a few aggressive herbs are mentioned is that some people like them enough to grow them despite their grievous faults. I confess that I'm going to keep growing chocolate and apple mint even though mint is a problem plant everywhere. But I do follow some planting rules to help corral invasive herbs, and I'm diligent about digging up excess plants.

Here are some strategies to lessen the impact of aggressive herbs:

- Grow herbs with invasive roots in containers. Put a screen over the drainage hole in the bottom of the pot. Raise the container off the ground so you can see and remove any roots that try to escape.
- For herbs that reseed too prolifically, remove all flowers before they begin to fade to prevent seeds from developing. Dispose of the flowers in the trash, not on the compost pile.
- Give aggressive herbs their own place that's far from other plants and where the soil is poor or heavy (has lots of clay).
- Plant herbs with wandering roots inside a metal, plastic, or wooden barrier sunk 1 to 2 feet into the ground. One easy way to do that is to sink a bottomless 5-gallon plastic bucket or 18-inch chimney flue liner into the soil so that about 2 inches of the rim sticks above the soil. Cover the soil surrounding the rim with pea gravel. Plant inside the bucket or flue liner.
- Grow mint in a hanging basket.
- Insert terra cotta roof tiles into the ground in a square or oblong box shape and plant herbs with mildly aggressive roots between the tiles.

Indoor Herb Growing

You may read cheerful references to growing herbs on kitchen windowsills over winter or potting up herbs from the garden and taking them indoors during cold weather. For many people, it isn't as easy as it sounds.

That's because kitchens don't usually have the amount of light most herbs require. Also, many of us conserve energy in winter by keeping the thermostat low, which doesn't please heat-loving herbs such as basil.

But it's certainly possible to grow some herbs indoors. The main thing is to provide plenty of light—in a sunroom or greenhouse, or under fluorescent lights. The problem with windowsills is that they get sun for only a few hours a day, generally not the 7 or more hours that most herbs need for good growth.

Increasing the humidity around the plants will also help them thrive. You can mist the plants, but placing pots atop pebbles in a shallow tray filled with water is the easiest way.

Use a regular potting soil and water whenever the top one-half inch of soil dries out. Fertilize monthly, unless your potting soil was

prepackaged with slow-release fertilizer. Possible pests might be spider mites, whiteflies, or mealybugs. Spray them with insecticidal soap (an organic control available at garden centers).

Herbs that do well indoors include bay, chervil, chives, marjoram, mint, oregano, parsley, rosemary, sage, tarragon, and thyme. 'Fernleaf' dill is worth a try. Be careful not to overwater the sage, which can mildew.

As long as you can provide enough light, herbs are a delightful winter project. They're much more fun than a philodendron or weeping fig— and tasty too.

How to Propagate Herbs

There are four simple methods of propagating, or reproducing, herbs in your garden so you'll have more. See the chart on page 21 to find the preferred technique for the herb you want to propagate. Here's what you need to know about each.

Seed

Not all herbs grow well from seed, and named cultivars won't come true from seed or produce a plant that's exactly like the parent. But for many herbs, it's the least expensive and easiest way to propagate a number of plants at once.

1. You can sow seeds indoors or outdoors. Indoors, you will need containers, potting soil, and labels.

2. Place the potting soil or starting medium in containers at least 3 inches deep and water until it's moist all the way through.

3. Sow seeds according to the depth recommended on the seed packet. Don't crowd them too close together!

4. Label the container with the name of the plant and the date the seeds were sown.

5. Keep the soil moist but not wet. Use tepid water, not cold.

6. Once the seeds have sprouted, give them light. Fluorescent fixtures ("shop lights") work well. You don't need a more expensive grow light.

7. Many potting mixtures contain fertilizer, but if young plants are grown indoors for more than 6 weeks in a plain mix, feed them very lightly with a balanced fertilizer.

8. Gradually introduce the plants to the conditions outdoors, so they're used to the sun, temperature, and wind by the time they're placed in the garden.

Cuttings

Late spring or early summer is a good time to take stem cuttings of herbs.

1. You'll need a pair of pruners, containers, potting soil, and rooting hormone.

2. Using clean, sharp pruning shears, take a cutting of a stem that is not flowering. The best place to cut is just above the lowest set of leaves. Make the cut on an angle.

3. Remove the lower leaves, leaving two sets of leaves at the top.
4. Dip the ends of the stems in rooting hormone.
5. With a pencil, poke a hole in the potting soil and insert the cutting carefully in it. Firm the soil around the stem.
6. Place in a warm, light place (not in sun). Rooting may take from 2 to 10 weeks. You'll know the cuttings have roots when they start to grow, or when you give them a slight tug and feel resistance.
7. If a cutting wilts, place a plastic bag over the container so it doesn't touch the cutting. That will hold in moisture.

Division

Another method is to dig up a plant and divide it into two or more smaller plants. This works well for herbs that form clumps. You may divide plants in spring or fall, but less-hardy herbs are best divided in spring.

1. Dig deeply all around the plant and pull up the rootball and attached soil.
2. With a knife, shovel, or two garden forks, separate the plant into smaller clumps. Make sure that each has a shoot and ample roots.
3. Replant and water.

Layering

This works best with herbs such as rosemary that have woody stems.

1. Bend a long, flexible shoot to the ground.
2. Make a small nick or wound in a spot that touches the soil. (Scrape a bit of the bark, but don't go all the way through.)
3. Cover the wounded area with soil.
4. Make sure the area stays in contact with the soil by securing it with a brick, rock, or wire pin.
5. Keep the soil moist.
6. When roots develop, cut the shoot off just below the roots and plant.

Best Ways to Propagate Herbs

Anise	Seed	Lamb's ears	Division
Anise hyssop	Seed, cuttings, division	Lavender	Cuttings, layering
Artemisia	Cuttings, division	Lemon balm	Seed, cuttings, division
Basil	Seed	Lemongrass	Division
Bay	Cuttings, layering	Lemon verbena	Cuttings
Bergamot (bee balm)	Division, cuttings (seed variable)	Licorice	Seed, division
Borage	Seed	Marjoram	Cuttings, layering, seed
Caraway	Seed	Mint	Division, cuttings
Catnip	Seed, cuttings, division	Mullein	Seed
		Nasturtium	Seed
Chamomile	Division, seed (not of cultivars)	Oregano	Cuttings, division
Chervil	Seed	Parsley	Seed
Chives	Seed, division	Pot marigold (calendula)	Seed
Cilantro/ Coriander	Seed	Rosemary	Cuttings, layering
Comfrey	Division, cuttings	Rue	Cuttings, division, layering
Dill	Seed		
Fennel	Seed	Sage (and other salvias)	Cuttings, division, layering, seed
Feverfew	Seed, cuttings, division	Salad burnet	Cuttings, layering
Garlic	Cloves	Savory, summer	Seed
Geranium, scented	Cuttings	Savory, winter	Cuttings, division
		Sweet woodruff	Division
Germander	Seed, cuttings	Tansy	Seed, division
Horehound	Seed, division	Tarragon	Division, cuttings
Horseradish	Division	Thyme	Division, cuttings, layering
Hyssop	Seed, cuttings, division	Violet	Seed, division
Lady's mantle	Seed, division	Yarrow	Seed, division

Grilling
Herb Garden

SHOPPING LIST

Basil
Chervil
Chives
Cilantro
Garlic
Onions
Oregano
Parsley
Rosemary
Sage
Tarragon
Thyme

In summertime, herbs are at their peak of flavor and freshness, and many of us cook outdoors on the grill several times a week. Why not combine the two with a grilling herb garden that's located close to the grill? Having a bounty of fresh herbs right at hand so you can reach over and snip off what looks good will add pizzazz to all your cookout favorites. Fish, seafood, chicken, steak, and burgers, as well as vegetables that love to be grilled, from corn to zucchini, will sizzle with extra flavor when you don't have to leave the grill to find your favorite herbs. And as you discover quick, creative ways to add more flavor to all your grilled foods, you'll find that everyone clamors for more. We won't tell your herbal secret!

Keep a pair of clippers or clean, sharp scissors with a big spatula and basting brush at the grill so you're always ready to snip a selection of culinary herbs to add a burst of flavor to your outdoor meals.

The Garden

For convenience, you'll want to grow your favorite herbs for grilling in a border beside the patio, in boxes attached to a deck's rails, in pots on your porch, or in a raised bed that's not far from your grill. Depending on your space, and the number of herbs you'd like to grow, you may want to take advantage of all these locations.

Consider a plant's size and form as well as leaf shape and color to determine which plants to place together. Rosemary is the tallest herb in the group and needs to be in the back of a border or grown in a large container, either by itself or with a border of shorter plants, such as parsley, around the edge.

Another design consideration is to group plants that need the same type of care. Basil, chives, cilantro, garlic, onions, parsley, and tarragon need regular watering, while oregano, sage, and thyme will happily grow in drier soil. Consider using golden oregano as a colorful border around them.

You may want to put the annual herbs, or those generally grown as annuals in most climates—basil, chervil, cilantro, garlic, onions, parsley, and rosemary—in containers since they will be killed by fall frost. Growing these in pots allows for easy cleanup and replanting the following spring. Containers are also good for those herbs that you'd like to grow inexpensively from seed. These include basil, chervil, chives, parsley, and green onions.

The most attractive way to plant a container is to place the tallest plant in the center (or the back, if the container isn't going to be moved), surround it with plants that are slightly shorter and have a different leaf form, and then have a trailing plant, or low-growing plant, that spills over the rim of the pot. For example, try one or two plants of purple-leaf basil (or tricolor sage) in the center, chives or garlic chives surrounding it, and thyme along the edge.

Smaller individual pots of herbs are a nice addition to a grilling garden too. These can be moved around easily and replaced when you've cut them back extensively. Chives, thyme, and parsley are good choices for smaller containers. Remember that parsley tolerates a fair amount of shade, so use it in your less sunny spots. The main drawback of container herb gardens is that their soil dries out faster than the ground, so they need watering regularly. (See page 16 for more about growing herbs in pots.)

An easy way to make an herb basting brush is to gather short stalks of fresh herbs and tie them to the end of the handle of a clean wooden spoon. Dip the herbs into a marinade and brush onto food as it cooks. After the meal, discard the herbs and wash the spoon; it will be ready to use again when needed.

If you don't have room to grow all the herbs listed, choose a few of your favorites. A basic grilling herb garden would start with basil, chives, parsley, sage, and thyme, with the addition of rosemary if you have room for a tall plant. If you're especially fond of growing rosemary and don't have too much space, choose a shorter cultivar. (In colder climates, where it's an annual, rosemary will naturally grow shorter.)

Gardeners who have plenty of space may want to make their grilling garden even more useful by adding a few heirloom tomato plants and some peppers—hot peppers as well as orange and yellow bell peppers. Remember that yellow summer squash and Delicata squash are wonderful when grilled. (Sprinkle them with your choice of basil, chives, oregano, or thyme. Delicious!)

Grilling with Herbs

You'll want to experiment with combinations of fresh herbs in marinades and dried herbs in rubs. But don't stop there.

- Cut stalks of rosemary and use them as flavorful skewers for grilling shrimp.
- Another way to make an herb basting brush is to gather stalks of herbs with stiff stems—thyme, rosemary, oregano, sage, or lavender—strip the leaves from the bottoms of the stalks, and tie together near the base. Then dip the top portion into a marinade and brush onto meats or veggies.
- Thread fresh herbs such as rosemary, sage, and thyme on skewers alternately with meat and veggies. Remove most of the foliage from 12-inch stalks of rosemary, sage, or other long-stemmed herbs. Leave a small tuft of leaves at one end. Soak in water for 15 to 30 minutes. Then thread veggies, shrimp, or chunks of chicken onto the herb stalks. (If necessary, pierce the food with a skewer first to make it easier to insert the herb stems.) Brush with olive oil and grill. This is a good use for herbs past their prime.
- Place herbs on top of the grate or mesh screen and put your meat or vegetables directly on the herbs. (If needed, use a grilling tray with small openings to prevent the herbs from falling into the fire.)
- Sprinkle fresh herbs (snipped finely) right on top of chicken, meat, fish, or vegetables.
- Place herbs such as oregano and sage on a piece of heavy-duty foil, and top with meat, chicken, or fish. Put more herbs on top of the food. Fold the foil into a packet and grill.

Grilled Pork Chops With Herbs

1 tablespoon finely chopped fresh rosemary
1 teaspoon dried herbes de Provence (see p. 159)
$^1/_2$ teaspoon salt
$^3/_4$ teaspoon freshly ground black pepper
2 cloves garlic, minced
4 boneless pork chops

In a small bowl, mix the rosemary, herbes de Provence, salt, pepper, and garlic. Spray both sides of the pork chops with nonstick cooking spray and rub with the herb mixture, pressing so it adheres. Place the chops in the refrigerator, covered, for 1 hour so they absorb the flavors. Grill over hot coals about 5 to 10 minutes per side, or until an instant-read meat thermometer registers 160 degrees. Yield: 4 servings.

All-Purpose Herb Rub For Grilling

2 tablespoons finely chopped fresh basil or
  2 teaspoons dried basil
1 tablespoon finely chopped fresh oregano or
  1 teaspoon dried oregano
1 tablespoon finely chopped fresh rosemary or
  1 teaspoon dried rosemary
2 teaspoons finely chopped fresh thyme or
  1 teaspoon dried thyme
1 tablespoon fennel seeds, crushed
1 teaspoon ground (dried) coriander
2 cloves garlic, finely minced, or 2 teaspoons garlic powder
1 tablespoon kosher or sea salt
2 teaspoons freshly ground black pepper

Combine all the ingredients in a bowl. Moisten the surface of meats or fish with olive oil or other liquid and rub both sides with the herb mixture. Refrigerate 15 to 60 minutes, then grill. (If you're using all dried herbs, this rub will keep in a covered jar at room temperature. If you're using fresh herbs, make just enough for a single use.) Yield: $^1/_2$ cup.

Pairing Herbs With Food

If you're not sure which herbs taste best with which foods, here's a quick guide to get you started. You'll soon discover many more ideas.

Basil—Tomatoes, chicken, salads
Chervil—Salads, vegetables, salad dressings
Chives—Beef, fish, potatoes, salads, tomatoes
Cilantro—To impart a Southwestern taste to meats and vegetables
Garlic—Beef, chicken
Onion—All meats and vegetables
Oregano—Meats, sauces
Parsley—Garnish, marinades, salads
Rosemary—Chicken, lamb, pork, potatoes, veal
Sage—Chicken, sausages, turkey
Tarragon—Fish, chicken, turkey, salad dressing
Thyme—All meats and most vegetables

Herb Marinade

¹/₄ cup olive oil
3 tablespoons Worcestershire sauce
3 teaspoons fresh minced garlic
1 tablespoon coarsely chopped fresh rosemary
1 to 2 tablespoons coarsely chopped fresh thyme
¹/₂ teaspoon freshly ground black pepper

Put the oil, Worcestershire sauce, garlic, rosemary, thyme, and pepper in a glass jar with a lid and shake to mix. Pour into a zipper-type plastic bag. Add meat or chicken and seal. Place in a refrigerator for at least 30 minutes, preferably several hours. Turn several times. Remove food from marinade and grill.
Yield: About ¹/₂ cup.

Potpourri
Herb Garden

Artemisia
Basil
Bergamot
Chamomile
Cilantro/
Coriander
Dianthus
Geranium,
scented
Lavender
Lemon balm
Lemon verbena
Marjoram
Mint ﹀
Nasturtium
Oregano
Pot marigold
Rose
Sage & salvias
Sweet
woodruff
Tansy
Violet

Fragrance is one of the most popular reasons for growing herbs, but those evocative aromas don't have to stay outdoors. Make potpourri and enjoy the sweet scent of herbs inside your house all year-round. It's easy—and fun—if you grow the right herbs. And you don't even need a garden; many herbs grow easily in containers. A potpourri garden also prevents waste—herbs that go into potpourri don't need to look perfect, as those for cooking or garnishing might. And you can create distinctive potpourris in fall by harvesting herbs still in the garden rather than letting them be killed by frost.

The Garden

A potpourri garden combines fragrant herbs and colorful flowers, so this is a garden that you'll want to grow where it can be seen and enjoyed.

An informal cottage garden can be quite effective for potpourri herbs. Although you won't have rows of herbs arranged from short in front to tall in back, you'll still want to keep in mind the mature sizes of plants as you plan where they will go. Be sure to read the labels of the specific plants you purchase, since various cultivars can grow to different heights. Different *Artemisia* varieties, for instance, can top out at 2 feet high—or 5 feet!

The tallest herbs in this garden are the roses, lemon verbena, and Sweet Annie artemisia. Bergamot and a few of the basils can easily reach 4 feet tall. The shortest plants will be dianthus, some cultivars of pot marigold, sweet woodruff, and violets. You may want to save these for edging.

Sweet woodruff and violets will enjoy a shady spot. If the location you've chosen for your potpourri garden is completely in full sun, place them where they'll be shaded by taller plants. Or grow them in containers so they can be moved to a shadier area and so they won't spread.

For easy care, group together the plants that need regular watering in an area with moist soil or that's near the hose: bergamot, chamomile, coriander, scented geraniums, marjoram, pot marigold, and sweet woodruff.

Another section of the garden could be home to the plants that prefer drier soil: artemisia, dianthus, lavender, lemon balm, nasturtium, sage and salvias, and tansy.

Most cottage gardens mix annuals and perennials together. But if you'd prefer to give them separate sections of the garden, these are annuals: basil, cilantro/coriander, scented geraniums, lemon verbena, most marjorams, nasturtium, and pot marigold.

Special care should be taken with mints, sweet woodruff, tansy, and violets, which may be invasive (mint is sure to be). See page 17 for how to handle them.

How to Make Potpourri

Dry the leaves, flowers, and seeds before you begin. (Since the flowers bloom at various times during the growing season, harvest and preserve them as they appear. Then store them until you're ready to make potpourri.)

A good way for a novice to start is with an equal amount of leaves and flowers, and toss in a few seeds. Place them all in a large bowl with a lid and mix in 1 to 2 tablespoons of fixative (see page 32) for each quart of dried plant material. Stir well, close the lid, and let the fragrance develop for 2 to 3 weeks. You may want to shake or stir the mixture a few times as it's drying, especially if you've used an essential oil (available at craft shops) in the mixture.

If the scent isn't strong enough for you after a few weeks, add a few drops of an essential oil and let the scent continue to develop for 10 to 15 days more. If you want, break up the potpourri into smaller pieces before storing it in sealed plastic bags or a covered container in a dark, dry place.

All the plants, including roses, may be grown in containers but will need watering more frequently.

If you don't have room for all the plants on the list, start with chamomile, scented geraniums, lavender, and lemon balm. Add a small rosebush if there's space.

Potpourri Ingredients

The plants in this sweet-smelling herb garden will allow you to create various scents of potpourri, depending on your preferences, the season, and where you'll use it. For instance, try a woodsy, more masculine scent for a man's den, or a light, citrusy potpourri for a closet sachet.

Potpourri needs a predominant scent, which can be herby (mint, marjoram), flowery (rose, lavender), spicy (whole cloves), woodsy (pine), or citrusy (orange peel), depending on its ingredients. You'll also want some complementary fragrances that blend with and enhance the main scent. Experiment and

find the combinations that are most pleasing to your nose. Or make a single-scent potpourri from scented geraniums, rose petals, or lavender. They're especially nice for sachets.

Generally, lavender and rose are the most versatile fragrances. They blend well with many different herbs. Most potpourri makers start with a basic recipe or idea and then add a bit of this and a bit of that to see what will develop.

Supplies and Equipment

You'll need a fixative such as orrisroot (available at craft stores), a large glass or stainless steel bowl, measuring cups and spoons, an eye dropper (if you use essential oils), and zipper-type plastic bags of various sizes to store the potpourri. A mortar and pestle is also a good investment if you make potpourri every year.

When you see them on sale or at a garage sale, you'll also want to stock up on interesting containers to hold and display your potpourri. Ideas include baskets, glass goblets, tins, large seashells, and vases.

Did you know that you can make your own essential oils? Place fresh herbs in a large glass or ceramic bowl. Pour a mild cooking oil (corn oil, safflower oil, and so forth) over the herbs until they're covered. Let the mixture sit for 24 to 36 hours and then strain, pressing the herbs against the strainer to release all their fragrance. Discard the herbs. Add more fresh herbs and flowers to the same oil and repeat the process 4 or 5 times. Place the oil in a tightly covered container and refrigerate.

Gifts From a Potpourri Garden

Basic Potpourri

2 cups dried herbs

2 cups dried flowers

1 teaspoon essential oil, optional

Geranium Sachet

2 cups scented geranium leaves (rose, mint, apple)

$^1/_2$ cup peppermint or spearmint leaves

1 tablespoon coriander seed

$^1/_4$ cup orrisroot

Mix the geranium and mint leaves, the coriander seed, and orrisroot in a non-reactive bowl (glass is good). Then transfer to an airtight container. Let the fragrances mingle for 2 to 3 weeks. Fill your sachet bags with the mix and tie each with a pretty ribbon. These are great gifts!

Potpourri Pillow

1 cup violet petals

$^3/_4$ cup rose petals

$^1/_2$ cup rosemary

3 to 4 tablespoons orrisroot

Combine the violet and rose petals, rosemary, and orrisroot in a small bowl or glass dish. Let the potpourri sit for 2 to 3 weeks so the aromas blend; you'll have to use an airtight container (or a ziplock bag). Then, sew the mixture into tiny cloth "pillowcases."

Flower Ice Cubes

Want to dress up lemonade, punch, or other cool beverages? Place an herb flower or even a single petal in an ice cube tray, fill with water, and freeze. Flowers that are pretty in ice cubes include borage, mint, lavender, and scented geranium. If you don't have any flowers on hand, use a leaf of pineapple sage or variegated mint.

Moth-Repellent Sachet

1 cup lavender leaves

$^1/_2$ cup mint leaves

$^1/_2$ cup southernwood (a type of artemisia)

Toss the lavender, mint, and southernwood leaves together in a ziplock bag or other airtight container. Set aside for 2 to 3 weeks. To make the sachets, fill small cloth or muslin bags with the moth-repellent and sew shut.

Night
Herb Garden

SHOPPING LIST

- Artemisia
- Bergamot (white flowering)
- Dusty miller
- Garlic chives
- Geranium, scented, 'Snowflake'
- Horehound
- Lamb's ears
- Lavender
- Mullein
- Rue
- Sage
- Sweet woodruff
- Yarrow
- Yucca

You spend time and effort creating a lovely garden and what happens? You really get to enjoy it only on the weekends, because you're at work the rest of the time, or off at the soccer field with the kids. Well, here's a garden that is best appreciated in moonlight—and that makes it great for after-dark entertaining too. This "evening garden" is filled with herbs that shimmer at night because they have silver or grayish foliage or white flowers.

Much of its appeal is that enjoying a garden seems unexpected after dark. Plants that are "ordinary" in daylight are considered more mysterious and intriguing at night. A night garden also engages the senses of sight and smell. You can add a third sense to that list too. Have you ever noticed that sounds are more noticeable at night? This garden is the perfect place for a tabletop fountain or a Japanese water flute.

The Garden

This is a garden you'll want to place near a deck, porch, or patio so you can catch the scent of the herbs as well as gaze at them in the twilight. That's a location that may not lend itself to a traditional garden, so you might consider planting a 2-foot border around the edges of a deck or placing the plants in a series of large pots, perhaps augmented by a few window boxes.

If possible, put a gazing ball somewhere in your night herb garden. You'll love how it shines under the moon and adds sparkle to the scene.

Except for bergamot and sweet woodruff, which need regular watering during the growing season, all of the plants in this evening garden need little extra moisture once they are established, making them especially easy-care for the busy gardener.

As you plan this garden to fit your available space, think about the plants' flowers, foliage, and scents as well as colors, form, and size. Place the plants grown primarily for their foliage—artemisia, dusty miller, lamb's ears, and sage—around and among the plants that bloom prolifically. Also keep in mind that perennial flowers will appear at different times during the growing season, depending on the plant. Scented geraniums, which are annuals, will bloom all summer long.

Adding Light to Your Night Garden

If you want your twilight herb garden to sparkle even more, add some low-voltage lights, which are economical to burn and can easily be installed by a handy homeowner. Some types to consider:

- **Fairy lights**
- **Solar path lighting**
- **Spot lighting (on a plant or group of plants that are at their best)**
- **Step lights**
- **Water garden or fountain lights**

Yucca is one of the tallest plants on our shopping list; it generally grows to about 8 feet, although various cultivars range from 18 inches high to 20 feet. Choose one that will fit your space. 'Color Guard' is a nice variegated yucca that grows about 2 feet tall and is said to be hardy to Zone 4. Be careful to place yucca so someone can't accidentally brush against its sharp spines.

Mullein also belongs in the back of the border, since its flower stalk tops out at 6 feet. Because mullein is a biennial, it will produce flowers only the second year, but reseeds itself so that before long, you will always have one blooming each year.

Place dusty miller and lamb's ears at the front of the border, since they're short. As annuals in most climates, both will need to be replanted each year.

Sweet woodruff, a low-growing deciduous ground cover, could also edge your beds, but it needs shade and may spread more than you like. Garlic chives are best grown in containers, since they can become invasive. All the other herbs range from 1 to 3 feet high—read the labels of the plants you buy to see how tall your cultivars will become at maturity—so you'll want to space them accordingly between the tall plants in the back and the short ones in the front.

Even if you don't have much outdoor space, you can still create a little nook that glows on midsummer nights.

Whatever the size of the planting, don't forget the most important element of all—comfortable seating to enjoy the sights and scents of your enchanting moon garden.

Winged Visitors to a Night Garden

Plants aren't the only attraction of a moon garden. Interesting winged guests may show up after dark to put on a surprise show. In the eastern half of the United States (and from Nova Scotia to Saskatchewan in Canada), one of the most fascinating is the luna moth (*Actias luna*).

These translucent green moths (see the illustration) are attracted to lights and mate only after midnight. They're members of the Giant Silkworm Moth family and have a wingspan up to 5 inches across.

Female luna moths lay their eggs during the night on trees that include hickory, persimmon, sumac, sweet gum, walnut, white birch, and willow. The green caterpillars that emerge from the eggs spin papery cocoons in leaf litter at the base of the trees. From these hatch new luna moths. There will be one to three new generations each year.

Although they're large, luna moths are as harmless as they are beautiful. Many of the plants that attract butterflies—moths' daytime cousins—also attract a variety of moths at night. (See page 49 for a list of herbs that attract butterflies.) The moths that show up depend on your region and the time of the year. More will be seen on cloudy nights when there's no wind.

Fragrant and Night-blooming Additions

Want to jazz up your evening garden even more? Consider interspersing a few special flowers among your herbs.

While any white-flowered or silver-foliaged plant would be okay, your garden will be truly magical after dusk when you add the plants on the list below that don't bloom during the day.

Scented flowers, such as fragrant roses, are also a charming part of a night herb garden because you can smell their sweet aromas nearby even when you can't see them. The ones recommended here combine both heady scent and white flowers that gleam in moonlight.

Fragrant Plants

- Butterfly bush (*Buddleia davidii*) with white flowers such as 'White Profusion'
- *Clematis henryi* (a vine)
- Flowering tobacco (*Nicotiana alata*)
- Gardenia (Zones 6 and warmer)
- Hosta 'Fragrant Dreams' (for shady areas)
- *Hosta plantaginea*
- Passionflowers (*Passiflora* spp. and hybrids)
- Snow on the Mountain (*Euphorbia marginata*)— May be invasive
- White cleome (*Cleome hassleriana*)
- White petunias
- White roses such as 'Moondance', 'Winchester Cathedral', 'Blanc Double de Coubert', or 'White Lightnin'

Plants That Bloom at Night

- Angel's trumpets (*Brugmansia arborea*)
- Evening primrose (*Oenothera biennis*)—May be invasive
- Moonvine (its white flowers are also fragrant)
- Night-blooming cereus (a houseplant except in frost-free areas)
- White four-o'clocks

Pizza
Herb Garden

Until someone comes up with a mozzarella plant, you can't grow your own pizza—but you can come close. Your backyard can produce the freshest ingredients possible, allowing you to create interesting toppings, a great pizza sauce, or to spice up a favorite store-bought sauce. To make the project even more fun, plant a round garden—24 to 48 inches in diameter—divided into "slices" to look like a pizza. Kids love the concept of a pizza garden and are eager to help—and eat what they've grown.

The Garden

If you can find an old wooden wagon wheel, place it in the garden and plant within its spokes. Another option is to use pieces of wood to create triangle-shaped raised-bed "slices" (this is an easier option that doesn't require you to dig up the ground). Or, border the pizza "slices" with bricks or pavers. Of course, you don't have to separate the different sections, but having the garden resemble a pizza is part of the fun.

This is a garden to plant in a spot that's in the sunshine all day, although parsley won't mind some shade if it's available. Take care to position the taller plants so they don't shade their shorter neighbors. Tomatoes will grow the tallest and will need some support—either stakes or metal cages. Some basils also reach up to 4 feet high, and in Zones 8 and warmer, where rosemary is perennial, basils can easily reach 5 feet tall. Peppers range from 1 to 3 feet in height. The rest of the recommended herbs and vegetables will top out at 1 to 2 feet.

To simplify care, place thyme and rosemary near each other, since they like less water than the other plants. You may also want to plant the perennials—thyme, chives, and, in warm climates, rosemary—in adjoining sections since they come back year after year and won't need to be replanted. Parsley is a biennial and will live 2 years, but many gardeners treat it as an annual and start fresh each spring; it can take some shade. All the rest are annuals and must be replanted each year. (Garlic is planted in fall.)

For a small pizza garden, you'll want: 2 basil plants, 2 chives, 1 cilantro, 3 to 5 garlic plants, 4 to 6 onions, 1 oregano, 1 parsley, 1 'Gypsy' bell pepper, 1 'Zavory' (or jalapeño) hot pepper, 2 rosemary plants, 1 thyme, 1 'Sungold' (or 'Super Sweet 100') cherry tomato, and 1 'Cherokee Purple' (or 'Brandywine') tomato. If your soil is poor or you are short on garden space, all of these, including the tomatoes, will grow in containers.

This garden is a fun way to experiment with varieties of tomatoes and peppers that are new to you. Kids are always intrigued by black tomatoes, which have a delightfully sweet flavor that belies their dark exterior, and striped tomatoes such as 'Tigerella'.

If you have room only for cherry tomatoes, consider the heirlooms 'Tiny Tiger' and 'Black Plum'. Both can be grown in containers to save space.

Although the peppers themselves may be too hot for many people, the 'Black Pearl' pepper plant is a colorful addition to any pizza garden because of its purplish-black foliage and red to black peppers. 'Calico' has leaves spotted green, white, and lavender and peppers that are yellow, purple, red, yellow, and white—that's some combination! The peppers don't have much flavor, but they'll be a colorful pizza addition nevertheless.

When picking, cutting, or cooking with hot peppers, always wear gloves and avoid touching your skin with the peppers, because they can cause a burning sensation. Be especially careful not to touch your face and eyes with hands that have touched hot peppers.

Although many cooks consider flat-leaf parsley superior for cooking, plant curly parsley if you have toddlers in the family— they love its little "trees."

In Greek, oregano means "joy of the mountain." The herb grows wild in the mountainous parts of the Mediterranean. Ancient Greek women used it as a perfume.

Basil is native to India, where it's considered a sacred herb to Hindus. English poet John Keats wrote a rather gory poem featuring basil: "Isabella, or the Pot of Basil."

Carlyle's Favorite Pizza

Prepared pizza dough
Pizza sauce, heavy on the basil and oregano
1 to 2 cups shredded low-fat mozzarella or
  fresh Parmesan cheese
10 cherry tomatoes or 1 regular tomato, seeded
1 cup chopped grilled chicken breast

Preheat the oven to 425 degrees F. Place the pizza dough in a greased pan and spread the sauce lightly over it to cover. Sprinkle the cheese on top. Halve the cherry tomatoes or chop the regular tomato and sprinkle over the cheese. Top with the grilled chicken and bake for 20 to 25 minutes. Makes one 12- to 16-inch pizza (6 to 8 servings).

Amy's No-Cook Pizza Sauce

1 (6-ounce) can tomato paste
1^1/$_2$ cups water
^{1}/$_3$ cup extra-virgin olive oil
2 teaspoons dried oregano
2 teaspoons fresh or frozen basil
^{1}/$_2$ teaspoon dried rosemary
2 cloves garlic, minced
Salt and freshly ground pepper to taste (optional)

Place the tomato paste, water, and oil in a medium bowl and blend well. Mix in the oregano, basil, rosemary, and garlic. (Double the amounts of all herbs, except basil, if you're using fresh herbs.) Taste the sauce and adjust the seasonings. Add salt and pepper, if desired. Cover the bowl and let it stand on the kitchen counter for 1 hour. Then refrigerate until needed. (This sauce improves if its flavors are allowed to mingle in the refrigerator for several hours before using.) Yield: about 2 ^{1}/$_2$ cups.

White Pizza

Prepared pizza dough

1 tablespoon butter or margarine

3 tablespoons flour

1 ¹/₄ cups milk

1 ¹/₂ teaspoons to 1 tablespoon minced garlic

1 ¹/₂ teaspoons freshly chopped basil

1 ¹/₂ teaspoons freshly chopped oregano

Salt and freshly ground black pepper to taste

¹/₄ to ¹/₂ cup shredded fresh Parmesan cheese

**Toppings (optional): sliced tomatoes; fresh basil leaves;
 chopped, cooked chicken breast**

Preheat the oven to 450 degrees F. Place the pizza dough in a large greased pan. Melt the butter in a medium saucepan over medium heat and add the flour. Stir together until thick but not brown (about 1 minute). Slowly add the milk, whisking constantly. Whisk in the garlic, basil, and oregano. (If using dried herbs, decrease the amount to ¹/₂ teaspoon each, or to taste.) Taste the sauce and season with the salt and pepper. Lower the heat if necessary to keep the sauce from sticking to the bottom of the pan. Simmer about 4 minutes, or until the mixture is thickened. Stir in the Parmesan cheese. Let the sauce cool slightly before spreading over the dough. Sprinkle with the toppings, if using, and bake about 20 minutes or until done. Yield: 1 ¹/₂ to 1 ²/₃ cups of sauce.

Butterfly
Bee, & Hummingbird
Herb Gardens

Add some living color to your herb garden by inviting butterflies, hummingbirds, and bees to visit and stay awhile. What's more enjoyable on a warm summer afternoon than watching tiny hummingbirds sip nectar from fire-engine-red bergamot flowers while gold and orange winged jewels flit from plant to plant, searching out nectar and host plants on which to lay eggs for the next generation. And don't forget bees, those essential pollinators of most of our fruits and vegetables. They've been having a tough time the past few years, so this is a good opportunity to help by providing a friendly habitat that's free of harmful chemicals.

Herbs That Provide Butterflies With Nectar

The suggested shopping list for a butterfly garden is already fairly long, but should you have room for more, here are more herbs that provide nectar for different kinds of adult butterflies:

Bergamot
Garlic chives (can be invasive)
Lavender
Tansy
Thyme

The Butterfly Garden

About half of the plants on the butterfly garden shopping list prefer dry soil and half need regular watering, so for ease of maintenance, group together those with similar needs. If you lack time or space to grow all the herbs on the shopping list, choose those that match your yard's conditions. Herbs that will be happy in dry soil are anise hyssop, borage, catnip, horehound, mullein, sage, summer savory, and yarrow.

If you'd prefer to concentrate on herbs that return year after year, the perennials are anise hyssop, catnip, chives, purple coneflower, fennel, horehound, mint, oregano, sage, winter savory, and yarrow. Mullein is a biennial that readily reseeds (sometimes to the point of being a pest), so it can be considered a perennial.

Mullein is the tallest of the group—its flower stalk shoots up to 6 feet tall—so place it where it won't interfere with other plants. Others that belong in the back of the bed because of their height are dill (although "dwarf" varieties are available) and fennel. Also, some cultivars of basil can grow up to 4 feet. Chives, marjoram, parsley, some sages, and winter savory are all candidates for edging a butterfly herb garden, or being placed in the front of a bed.

If possible, grow at least 3 of each plant—clumps of flowers are more likely to attract the butterflies than single flowers dotted here and there. And place host plants such as dill, fennel, and parsley among the flowering herbs that provide nectar. (You can read more about this below.)

If space is limited, you can limit your butterfly garden to a small collection of anise hyssop, horehound, oregano, purple coneflower, and yarrow. Or grow some of the annuals in containers, such as basil, borage, marjoram, and summer savory.

In fall, when the flowers in your butterfly herb garden fade, consider leaving the seeds on the plants for wild birds to eat. That way, you've helped butterflies and birds with the same garden. It's an environmental win-win.

Attracting Butterflies

- Make sure that at least one plant is in bloom from spring to fall, not just in summer.
- Choose flowers in a variety of hues—the brighter the better, since butterflies love colorful blossoms.
- Provide a mix of plants that produce needed nectar and that serve as host plants on which the butterflies will lay their eggs. When it comes to host plants, which the caterpillars will munch on, be sure to grow enough for you and them.
- Include a mud puddle or damp sand so the butterflies can drink.
- Provide a rock to sunbathe on.
- Practice organic gardening. Butterflies are extremely sensitive to any kind of chemicals.

Provide Plants for Butterflies' Entire Life Cycle

It's natural to want to attract colorful butterflies to our gardens, but sometimes we forget that these flying beauties do more than just flit around and sip nectar from pretty flowers.

Their main purpose in life is to reproduce so they also look for certain plants on which to lay eggs. These are called "host plants." When caterpillars hatch from the eggs, they will munch on the leaves of the plants, which sometimes makes a gardener unhappy. But it's a minor inconvenience to put up with a few bedraggled-looking plants for a time so that the caterpillars eat and grow, shedding their skin several times along the way before transforming into a chrysalis from which a new butterfly hatches.

SHOPPING LIST FOR BUTTERFLY GARDEN

Anise hyssop

Basil

Borage

Catnip

Chives

Coneflower, purple

Dill

Fennel

Horehound

Marjoram

Mint

Mullein

Oregano

Parsley

Sage

Savory, summer

Savory, winter

Yarrow

So instead of just planting herbs and flowers that are nectar sources for *adult* butterflies, it's good to observe which plants provide food sources for the various life stages. Mint, for instance, provides nectar for numerous butterflies, including the painted lady, red admiral, and monarch. Parsley is a host plant for two types of swallowtails. Dill and fennel are also host plants for the black swallowtail.

It's best to plant host and nectar plants near each other so that after the young butterflies hatch on the host plants they don't have to go far to feed.

The Hummingbird Garden

Sure, you can attract hummingbirds with sugar water dyed red, but providing their natural diet is so much better and prettier. Before you plant, plan a complementary color scheme for your hummingbird garden. All the recommended sages have red flowers. Anise hyssop has blue or purplish flower stalks, and bergamot's more rounded blooms come in red, magenta, pink, purple, and white. Use white and blue blooms to separate all the shades of red. Not only will that produce a pretty picture, it will give you a red, white, and blue patriotic theme.

Another design consideration is to group plants that need the same type of care. All need full sun. Bergamot requires more water than the other plants, so place it within easy reach of the hose. At the other end of the watering spectrum, anise hyssop can go in your driest spot. The sages are in between, requiring water during dry spells, especially when they're young, but they're relatively drought-tolerant. Still, they won't bloom well if not watered during a dry spell.

Anise hyssop and bergamot are perennials, but the others should be treated as annuals colder than Zone 8. Texas sage often reseeds itself, though, acting like a perennial.

These are generally tall plants—anise hyssop and Texas sage are the "short" plants at 2 to 3 or 4 feet tall. Bergamot reaches maturity at 3 to 4 feet. Hummingbird sage (or blue anise sage, as it's sometimes called) and pineapple sage can easily become 3 to 5 feet tall, although they probably won't reach their full mature height when grown as annuals.

If you really want a plant to make an impression, consider *Salvia guaranitica* 'Black and Blue', which has clear blue flowers on a plant that grows to 6 feet high. It's spectacular!

In a container hummingbird herb garden, all of the plants should do well if you choose large pots. Consider planting a big terra cotta container with 1 or 2 of each of the plants and placing it near your deck or patio, where you can watch the miraculous hummingbirds hover in a blur over the blossoms, rotating their wings in a circle.

Attracting Hummingbirds

- Provide plants with colorful flowers that produce plenty of nectar. Although red is hummingbirds' favorite color, they are attracted to other colors too. What these tiny birds really want is blooms that are good sources of nectar.
- Install a red or purple gazing ball near the hummingbird garden.
- A nectar feeder may initially entice hummers to your garden, especially before the plants have begun to flower. Buy one with an ant, hornet, and wasp guard.
- Garden organically. Not only is this good for the birds, but it means that some insects will stay in your garden and be an additional food source for the hummingbirds. (Hummers can consume large quantities of insects, which is an excellent reason for having them in your garden.)
- Provide a source of water—moving water, such as a fountain or mister—near the plants grown for the hummers.
- Shrubs, vines, and poles placed near your hummingbird-attracting herbs will give the birds somewhere to perch and rest or hide from possible predators when not visiting your flowers. Providing those as well as flowers also will entice hummers to build their nests in your yard.

SHOPPING LIST FOR SMALL HUMMINGBIRD GARDEN

Anise hyssop

Bergamot

Chives

Sage, hummingbird (*Salvia guaranitica*)

Sage, pineapple

Sage, Texas (*Salvia coccinea*)

Yarrow

The Bee Garden

When bees visit your yard, they are looking for pollen and nectar. So the recommended herbs include those that are good sources of both. Consider planting it cottage-garden style around a traditional straw bee skep.

The shortest plants are chamomile, chives, marjoram, oregano, many sages, and thyme. Anise hyssop, some basils, bergamot, catnip, some sages and salvias, and yarrow generally grow 3 to 4 feet. The others range from 1 ½ to 2 ½ feet high at maturity. Check the labels of the plants you buy, or the back of the seed packet to find the height for the cultivars you've chosen.

This will be a garden in full sun. To make maintenance easier, group together the plants that prefer dry soil—borage, catnip, lavender, sages and salvias, thyme, and yarrow—in one spot and the rest, which need regular watering, in a section of the yard with soil that stays moist or can easily be watered regularly.

All of the suggested plants are perennials except basil, borage, marjoram, and some salvias. For a container, try a plant of anise hyssop in the middle, pineapple sage around it, and chamomile along the pot's rim. Or, a white-flowered cultivar of bergamot in the center, lavender around it, and pink- or white-flowered thyme along the edges.

Other Herbs That Attract Bees

If you have space, here a few more herbs that attract bees:

Chives, Comfrey, Fennel, Rosemary

Other Plants for a Bee Garden

Although the list of herbs that attract bees and other pollinators is substantial, if you want to add a few flowers to your herb garden, here are some to consider:

Black-eyed Susan

Clematis

Lupine

New England aster

Sedum

Sunflower

Zinnia

**SHOPPING LIST
FOR
BEE GARDEN**

Anise hyssop
Basil
Bergamot
Borage
Catnip
Chamomile
Hyssop
Lavender
Lemon balm
Marjoram
Mint
Oregano
Sage & salvias
Thyme

For a small bee garden, the must-haves are bergamot and lavender. If space allows, add pineapple sage or a fruit-scented sage, two salvias that appeal to hummingbirds too.

Attracting Bees

- Have flowers blooming from spring through fall.
- Plant herbs in clumps of at least three, instead of singly. A 3-foot-diameter clump attracts more bees than individual plants here and there.
- Bees are attracted to color, so choose herbs with blooms in a variety of colors. Bee favorites include yellow, blue, and purple, with purple or lavender the hands-down choice when it's available.
- Plant the herbs in sunny areas, which bees are more likely to visit than shade. They also like a spot that's protected from high winds.
- Include flowers of different shapes, which will attract different types of bees.

Feverfew's strong odor repels bees so don't grow it near plants that need bees to pollinate them, such as tomatoes.

Kids'
Herb Gardens

Herbs are the perfect plants for introducing kids to gardening because they appeal to so many senses. The interesting shapes of the plants as well as their leaves and flowers—think dill and mullein, as well as parsley—make them fun to look at. And who could walk through an herb garden without reaching out to touch this plant and that, to feel the various textures, from soft and fuzzy to bristly? Of course, one of the main appeals of an herb garden is its many different aromatic opportunities, with fragrances that vary from sharp and spicy to soft and fruity. Herbs offer another plus for children (or their parents) who have little or no experience with gardening: they're generally easy to grow. Here are a few simple herb gardens whose themes will appeal to youngsters.

SHOPPING LIST

FOR A PETER RABBIT GARDEN

Beans
Blackberries
Cabbages
Chamomile
Cucumbers
Lettuces
Onions
Parsley
Peas
Potatoes
Radishes
Rosemary
Tansy
Thyme

Peter Rabbit Garden

Unless you have a large garden, re-creating Mr. McGregor's plot in Beatrix Potter's *The Tale of Peter Rabbit* may be too much. But it can be fun to reread the story with your children or grandchildren and let them decide which of the veggies and herbs mentioned would be fun to grow. All need full sun, except parsley, which will manage in some shade. Potatoes, peas, cabbages, lettuces, and radishes are usually planted in early spring while the others are set out after the chance of frost has passed, since they need warm weather. Unless you already have a garden spot dug up and ready to be planted, you may want to concentrate on the warmth-loving herbs and vegetables the first year, although a school class may want to go with the cold-tolerant crops since they will grow, and sometimes can be harvested, before school lets out for the summer.

If you have a spot with dry soil or that's far from a water spigot, plant tansy there. All of the other plants will need regular watering. The plants in this garden are mostly annuals and will need to be replanted each year. The exceptions include chamomile, from which Peter's mom brewed a tea for him after his big adventure. It's a perennial that will come back year after year. Parsley will live two years, but performs best its first year, so many gardeners treat it as an annual. Blackberries, which produce long canes, take up quite a lot of space and should go in a spot of their own. They also are perennials.

Those who have ample garden space may want to plant pole beans, which kids *love*. (See the bean teepee on page 59.) Otherwise, bush beans will save space. Cucumbers will need some supports on which to climb. Consider planting a mesclun mix for the lettuce, since it offers such a variety of shapes, colors, and tastes. Or try a red-leaf lettuce, since many children don't realize that lettuce isn't always green.

Are your kids interested in how Peter's chamomile tea tasted? It's easy for them to sample it themselves.

Peter Rabbit's Chamomile Tea

Bring 3 cups of water to a boil on the stove or in the microwave. Add 3 tablespoons dried chamomile flowers and 6 whole cloves and stir. If you boiled the water on the stove, remove the pan from heat and cover it. Let the mixture steep 15 to 20 minutes. Strain and sweeten with sugar or honey.

Edible-Flower Herb Garden

Borage, Chives, Garlic chives, Nasturtium

It's a treat for kids to discover that it's not just the leaves of herbs and other plants that we eat. Many of their flowers are also edible. The blooms of the herbs listed here are fun to taste and to add to salads or to serve as garnishes to vegetables or meat. Borage and nasturtiums like drier soil, while the two chives need regular watering. All will grow in containers. Consider planting both types of chives in a large container— they'll bloom at different times—placing the nasturtium around the edges of the pot, where it can trail over the rim. Give borage its own pot—remember that it can get to be about 3 feet tall—and tell children how, long ago, this cucumber-flavored herb was a favorite of ancient warriors, who used it to give them courage.

Tutti-Frutti Herb Garden

Geranium (orange-scented)
Lemon balm
Pineapple sage

Think about giving each plant its own container so that youngsters can concentrate on one scent at a time. Scented geraniums will sprawl and take up more space than you might expect so make sure the container is wide enough. Pineapple sage starts out small but take off once hot weather hits. Because regular lemon balm plants can be floppy and not necessarily attractive, choose a plant with variegated green-and-white leaves. It looks better in the garden. You may be able to find a number of scented geraniums with fruity scents to carry out this theme. Apple is a popular one. So, if you like, you could have a tutti-fruitti herb garden with just scented geraniums.

Minty Treats

Apple mint
Chocolate mint
Peppermint

When is a mint more than a mint? When it has another flavor too. This should be a container garden because mints send their roots out all over the garden and beyond, becoming pests in the process.

Mints prefer to grow in full sun, but manage quite nicely in partial shade. Be prepared to water them when the soil's surface dries out. Since mints are perennial and will come back the next year, you may want to plant them in wooden tubs or troughs, which are less likely to be unfavorably affected by winter weather than clay containers. Cut the plants frequently to keep them looking their best. Let the kids munch on the fresh cuttings and see if they can distinguish the chocolate mint or the apple mint from peppermint (or spearmint, which is often just sold as "mint"). Then show the children how chewing on mint leaves freshens the breath naturally.

A Salad in a Pot

Chives, Lettuce, Pepper, Tomato 'Sungold'

Some kids aren't fond of salads, but when you plant and care for your own plants, often a salad becomes a real treat. This one can be grown in two good-sized containers. Place a couple of plants of chives and several plants of leaf lettuce (which is very simple to start from seed) in one pot and a pepper and the 'Sungold' tomato in another. Keep them well watered. You'll need to provide a cage or some stakes for the tomato plant. The chives are perennial and can be repotted and taken indoors over winter, or left out in the garden to come up again the next spring. You'll have a wide selection of pepper plants from which to choose—tiny hot peppers for kids who like spicy food, banana peppers, and bell peppers of several different colors. (Orange is always fun.)

A Bean Teepee

Place wooden stakes in a teepee shape and fasten them together at the top. Plant pole beans seeds (such as 'Kentucky Wonder') at the base of each stake or pole. When the plants cover the stakes, they make a cool green tent in which a child will delight in hiding. If you have the space, make this the centerpiece of the Peter Rabbit garden. On hot days, water the bean teepee with a sprinkler, so that those inside will be "rained on."

More Ideas for Kids' Gardens

See the zoo herb garden (page 160), the sunflower herb house (page 160), the salsa garden (page 159), and the Italian garden (page 158), which you could call it a "spaghetti garden." Other theme gardens that have kid appeal include the alphabet garden (page 162), the rainbow herb garden (page 162), and the Harry Potter herb garden (page 163), which could be presented as a garden that might have grown at Hogwarts. That one would be for older children who understand that the "spells" and evil spirits aren't real. The bee, butterfly, and hummingbird gardens (pages 46-53) will also be of special interest to youngsters. Introducing children to butterflies and hummingbirds up close can start them on a lifelong love of nature.

Culinary
Herb Garden

Many people have become interested in growing herbs simply because they like to use them in the kitchen. And you needn't be a gourmet cook to realize that you can grow a selection of herbs in a pot near your back door and have fresh herbs from spring to fall for much less than it costs to buy a couple of packets of fresh herbs at the supermarket, which last only a few days. And the selection of plants you can grow is so much wider and more interesting. When you see a recipe that calls for an unusual herb, you will no longer have to hesitate to try it. You can confidently increase your culinary repertoire because you know you have the herbs you need right in your garden.

The Garden

Because many herbs are so good for cooking, a culinary herb garden can be as large as you have space for. The only requirement is that it be placed as close to the kitchen as possible so you can run out and snip what you need while you're in the middle of preparing a meal, if you want to.

Add pizzazz to your next picnic or cookout: use the hollow stems of sweet fennel as straws for lemonade and other cool summer beverages.

If your garden space is more limited, you'll want to shorten the list to a more manageable size by asking yourself:

- Which herbs do I use most often in cooking? Which others intrigue me, and are they some I want to add to my repertoire? Are they readily available from a neighbor or inexpensively at a grocery store?

- Do I want to plant most of the herbs once and have them come back in coming years? If so, the perennials on the Shopping List are: chives, fennel, garlic chives (which may be invasive), marjoram, mint (also likely to be aggressive), oregano, sage, salad burnet, winter savory, tarragon, and thyme. Rosemary is perennial for those who in Zones 8 and warmer, while lemongrass is perennial in Zones 9 and 10. Bay needs a frost-free climate but it may be grown in a pot and taken indoors to a sunny spot during winter.

- Am I interested in growing herbs mostly in pots placed conveniently near the back door? While garlic isn't ideal for container growing, most of the other plants are, even tomatoes if you put them in a large container. Plants that are right at home in containers include basil, both kinds of chives, mint, oregano, peppers, rosemary, sage, and thyme. Remember that containers will often need daily watering during hot summers.

- Is my soil dry or does it stay relatively moist? Lemongrass, sage, salad burnet, and thyme prefer dry soil and rosemary needs watering only during dry spells, unless they're grown in a container.

- Do I have room for a few big plants? Lemongrass and heirloom tomatoes ('Mr. Stripey' and 'Black Russian', for instance) will need more space. They'll take up less room if grown in 24-inch-diameter cages made from concrete reinforcing wire.

Once you've made up your mind which of the herbs will have a home in your culinary garden—and, because so many are annuals, the choices can change from year to year—think about how to place them.

The tallest plants are bay, dill, fennel, lemongrass, rosemary (where it's perennial; it will be shorter as an annual), and tomatoes. The shortest are chives, marjoram, oregano, parsley, sage, winter savory, and thyme, although the exact height of all the plants depends on the cultivars you grow.

To add interest to the garden, you may want to repeat several clumps of the culinary herbs you use the most in various parts of the garden—maybe parsley, chives, basil, sage, and thyme. There are many different cultivars of each of these, which will provide some variety in the garden and in your cooking.

The Most Popular Culinary Herbs

Basil

Chives

Cilantro/Coriander

Dill

Oregano

Parsley

Sage

Thyme

French Lessons

Traditionally, the classic French seasoning known as *fines herbes* was made with equal parts tarragon, chervil, parsley, and chives, although many cooks nowadays add other herbs. The herbs may be used either fresh or dried. In both cases, add them near the end of cooking to preserve their flavors.

Bouquet Garni

As with *fine herbes*, the seasoning known as bouquet garni has a number of variations. The classic recipe contains varying amounts of thyme, parsley, and bay leaf, which are placed in a small bag made from cheesecloth and tied at the top. The bag is then dropped into a soup, stew, or casserole to infuse the dish with flavor. Here are two traditional bouquet garni recipes—one using fresh herbs and one using dried—and a recipe that includes additional flavors.

Fresh Bouquet Garni

1 bay leaf

4 sprigs fresh parsley

4 sprigs fresh thyme

Dried Bouquet Garni

$^1/_4$ cup dried parsley

2 tablespoons dried thyme

2 tablespoons dried, crumbled bay leaf

(or 1 whole bay leaf)

Bouquet Garni Plus

1 teaspoon dried, crumbled bay leaf

$1^1/_4$ teaspoons dried marjoram

1 teaspoon dried parsley

$^1/_2$ teaspoon dried sage

$^1/_2$ teaspoon dried savory

$1^1/_2$ teaspoons celery seed (optional)

4 peppercorns (optional)

Horseradish Salad Dressing

$^1/_4$ teaspoon freshly grated horseradish

1 clove garlic, finely minced

1 teaspoon minced fresh basil

1 teaspoon minced fresh dill

1 teaspoon minced fresh parsley

$^1/_4$ cup red wine vinegar

2 teaspoons lemon juice

$^1/_4$ teaspoon soy sauce

$^1/_2$ cup extra-virgin olive oil

Place the horseradish, garlic, basil, dill, and parsley in a glass jar with a lid. Pour in the vinegar, lemon juice, soy sauce, and oil. Shake well to mix. Store in the refrigerator. Yield: about $^3/_4$ cup.

Herb Mayonnaise

1 cup mayonnaise (low-cal works fine), chilled
1 tablespoon chopped fresh basil
1 tablespoon chopped fresh chives
1 tablespoon chopped fresh dill
1 tablespoon chopped fresh oregano
1 tablespoon chopped fresh parsley

Place the mayonnaise in a small mixing bowl and add the basil, chives, dill, oregano, and parsley, blending well. Refrigerate any leftovers and use the next day. Yield: about 1 cup.

Parsley Butter

1 stick ($^1/_2$ cup) butter, softened
2 cups fresh parsley, minced
1 tablespoon lemon juice

In a small bowl or container, cream the butter until smooth. Mix in the parsley until well blended. Mix in the lemon juice. Store in the refrigerator. Spread a dollop on a hot steak or roast and let it melt—*yum!* Store in the refrigerator for up to 3 days. Yield: about 1 cup.

For the best flavor, add herbs to stews and casseroles during the last 15 or 20 minutes of cooking.

Simple Pesto

3 cups fresh basil leaves
1$^1/_2$ cups chopped walnuts or pine nuts
1 to 4 cloves garlic, peeled
$^1/_4$ cup grated Parmesan cheese
1 cup extra-virgin olive oil
Salt and freshly ground black pepper, to taste

In a food processor or blender, blend the basil, nuts, garlic, and Parmesan cheese. Pour in the oil slowly while still processing. Taste the pesto and add salt and pepper as desired. Use immediately or store for later use. To store, pour into a glass or plastic container with a lid and cover the surface with plastic wrap. Put the lid on the container and refrigerate. Yield: about 3 cups.

Easy Scented Geranium Cake

Cakes made with scented geraniums have been around at least since Victorian times. Some add scented geranium foliage to a traditional pound cake recipe or a variation of a pound cake recipe, such as the popular 7-Up pound cake. This recipe gives you the same aroma and flavor without as much effort.

1 package white or yellow cake mix (a size that makes 2 layers)

10 or 12 fresh rose-scented geranium leaves or lemon-scented geranium leaves

Grease two 8- or 9-inch cake pans, or spray with nonstick vegetable spray. Cut parchment paper to fit the bottoms and grease or spray them. Arrange clean and dry scented geranium leaves, top side down, over the parchment paper.

Preheat the oven to 350 degrees F.

Mix the cake according to package directions, adding eggs, oil, and any other ingredients called for. Carefully pour the batter over the geranium leaves and bake according to package directions.

Remove pans from oven when a tester comes out clean and let the layers cool on a wire rack for 10 minutes. Remove the cakes from pans and discard the geranium leaves. Let the layers cool to room temperature on a rack.

Frost with your favorite white or cream cheese icing, decorating the top of the cake with fresh scented geranium leaves or flowers. Yield: 8 to 10 servings.

Herb Jelly

2 cups fresh herbs of your choice (suggestions: basil, pineapple sage, lemon thyme, lemon verbena)
2 cups water
2 tablespoons plain rice vinegar
Pinch salt
3 $\frac{1}{2}$ cups sugar
3 ounces liquid pectin

Wash and sterilize 4 half-pint (8-ounce) jelly jars with 2-piece lids.

Wash and drain the herbs, then coarsely chop them. Place in a medium saucepan and use the bottom of a glass or a large wooden spoon to crush the herbs. Add the water and bring to a boil over low heat. Boil 10 seconds *only*. Remove the pan from the heat, cover, and let stand 15 minutes.

Pour the mixture through a strainer and then strain 1 $\frac{1}{2}$ cups of the liquid a second time into a large, deep pan. Add the rice vinegar, salt, and sugar. Stirring constantly, bring the liquid to a rolling boil over medium heat. When you can't stir down the boil, add the pectin. Let the mixture return to a rolling boil that can't be stirred down and boil for 1 minute, but no longer.

Remove the pan from heat. Skim the foam from the surface, discarding it; pour the liquid into the prepared, hot jelly jars, leaving one-half inch of head space (between the top of the liquid and the rim of the jar). Immediately seal with the 2-piece lids. Store in a cool, dry place. Yield: 4 half-pint jars.

This recipe is adapted from one by Renee Shepherd of Renee's Garden seeds.

Fragrance & Aromatherapy
Herb Garden

Aromatherapy, a practice dating back to antiquity, is the use of various fragrant plant oils (and byproducts such as rosewater) to change a mood and enhance well-being. Some herbs possess aromas that have a stimulating effect while others tend to relax us. When you grow herbs for aromatherapy, you're ready for whatever your day brings. If you prefer the outdoors to smell delightful as well as be beautiful, a fragrance garden is for you. Herbs offer so many pleasant and enticing scents. Most are used to attract pollinators, but—fortunately for us—are as pleasing to people as they are to bees, butterflies, and other insects.

SHOPPING LIST

AROMATHERAPY GARDEN

Basil

Bergamot

Chamomile

Geranium, rose-scented

Hyssop

Lavender

Marjoram

Mint, peppermint

Rosemary

Sage, clary

Thyme

FRAGRANCE GARDEN

Artemisia, 'Powis Castle'

Mint

Geranium, scented

Nicotiana

Rose

Sage & salvias

Sweet woodruff

Thyme

The Aromatherapy Garden

An aromatherapy garden is one with double benefits—it can make a pleasant refuge outdoors as well as provide herbs whose scents make you feel better. Who could be down in the dumps while the aroma of mint or lavender fills a room?

To enhance the beauty of your aromatherapy garden, group plants with flower colors in mind. Start with the rose, and choose it for the fragrance of its flowers ('Fragrant Delight' or maybe a climbing rose like 'Rosa Mulliganii' or 'Climbing Iceberg') and then select the other plants in complementary colors. Lavender will go well with pink or white roses, and so will Clary sage, which may have white or lavender blooms. Bergamot flowers come in shades of pink or red and in white. Tiny thyme blossoms are also pink, white, or red. There are several rose-scented geraniums and numerous mints, but most have pink or white blooms. Marjoram also flowers in pink or white, while hyssop is available with blue, pink, or white flowers. With its daisylike blooms, chamomile is a good choice next to a yellow rose.

For easy care, plant the herbs that like dry soil—lavender, Clary sage, and thyme—together and place the rest, which will need to be watered more frequently, in soil that holds moisture well but doesn't stay wet. To minimize time spent watering, consider positioning a

soaker hose or drip irrigation at the base of the roses and other plants that need regular watering. Not only is it efficient, it saves water—and money—and delivers moisture right where the plants need it, at the base. (When watering roses, avoid getting their leaves wet, which can sometimes lead to fungus diseases such as blackspot.)

You'll probably want to grow peppermint or other mints in containers on the edge of a aromatherapy garden to avoid their invasive spreading.

The Fragrance Garden

The fragrance garden has some of the same plants as those used for aromatherapy and can also be color-coordinated. But the focus should be picking the most fragrant varieties of each plant and growing complementary scents near one another. This will mean buying your plants in person, instead of by mail order, so your nose can make the decisions for you.

Mints, scented geraniums, decorative salvias, and thyme come in a wide variety of "flavors," so if you have the space, get several of the different fragrances that appeal to you most. Then choose the rose's fragrance to go with the predominant scents of the other plants. You could even double the rose aroma in the garden by growing rose-scented geraniums at the base of a rosebush.

Nicotiana is an annual flower often called flowering tobacco. Its flowers may be lavender, pink, red, white, or yellow and their very fragrant scent is strongest at night. It's an excellent choice for containers, but in the ground, looks better massed or in a grouping of at least three plants. Nicotiana will happily grow in partial shade.

Place thyme and artemisia in an area of the garden that has dry soil and watch out for artemisia's invasive tendencies. Creeping thyme will grow nicely between steppingstones or in the crevices of an old stone wall.

Don't forget to place some comfortable seating in the fragrance garden. You and your guests will want to take advantage of being surrounded by the plants' heady natural perfumes, which will change from day to day.

Add Heat for the Strongest Scent

To maximize the potential of a fragrance garden, you need two more things beyond plants: heat and touch. You'll notice the pleasant aromas of herbs more when the weather's hot and also when you touch or brush against the plants. For that reason, it's a good idea to place herbs with especially fragrant leaves or flowers in places where people are like to interact with them—next to a path or patio, or between steppingstones in a path.

Warmth and pressure release the scent of herbs. The plants will have a more discernable fragrance in warmer weather and also when you touch them or brush against them. That's why herbs such as thyme grown between steppingstones are such an olfactory delight in summer when you step on them.

Using aromatherapy, an herb grower might place certain herbs (or their oils) in bathwater to create an atmosphere of relaxation after a long, hard day. Or if she didn't sleep well the night before, she might skip her morning shower and instead indulge in a bath infused with herbs known for their invigorating aromas. Science is looking into whether this practice has a sound basis, but many people like the idea of using natural plant fragrances to soothe or uplift their spirits.

Herbs That Soothe and Relax

Chamomile

Geranium, rose-scented

Hyssop

Lavender

Marjoram

Rose flowers

Sage, Clary

Herbs That Invigorate

Basil

Bay

Bergamot

Mint, peppermint

Rosemary

Thyme

A Minty Bath

For a relaxing, fragrant bath, place several (washed) stems of mint under the hot water faucet for a few minutes when filling your tub. Or pour a pot of brewed mint tea (strained) into the bath.

Other Fragrant Plants

If you'd like to expand your fragrance garden beyond herbs, here are some sweet-smelling plants to consider.

Carolina allspice

Clethra (summersweet)

Dianthus (clove pinks)

Heliotrope

Hyacinth

Lilac

Linden tree

Lily-of-the-valley (may be invasive)

Mock orange

Sweet alyssum

Sweet pea

Pickling
Herb Garden

If you like pickles, you'll be amazed at how easy it is to make tasty pickles—from bread-and-butter slices to dills—at home. The taste is superior to and more interesting than supermarket pickles.

If you're a vegetable gardener, you'll find that a wide variety of popular veggies can easily be pickled: asparagus, beans, beets, okra, peppers, and many more. Often these are sold in jars at gourmet stores. But when you can so easily make your own in summertime, think of it as an inexpensive way to create a distinctive appetizer that's ready for serving all year. And the pickled veggies make great gifts too.

Don't worry that making your own pickles means buying a canner and all the equipment that goes with it. Many pickles can easily be made without canning; they "pickle" in the fridge.

The Garden

A pickling herb garden can be as small or as ambitious as you like. Maybe you'll want it to be a separate garden, with cucumbers growing on a fence or other support, with dill nearby and the peppers, garlic, and onions at their feet. Unless you live in a frost-free climate, the bay will have to be in a big pot that's taken indoors over winter.

You can save space by growing cucumbers up a metal tomato cage and tucking everything except the bay tree into a vegetable garden, if you have one. A vegetable garden is handy if you want to pickle a variety of veggies. That way, they'll all receive the full sun and regular watering they require and will be in the same place for harvesting.

If you don't have a vegetable garden and are short on space, that's no reason to give up on a pickling garden. Save room by growing all the plants in good-sized containers. Because regular dill is generally too tall for container growing, use a dwarf variety such as 'Fernleaf'.

Sally's Microwave Pickles

This is a handy recipe for times when you're out of pickling cucumbers, but have regular ones.

1 medium cucumber, thinly sliced

2 small onions, thinly sliced

$^3/_4$ cup sugar

1 teaspoon salt

$^1/_2$ teaspoon celery seed

$^1/_2$ teaspoon mustard seed

1 tablespoon chopped fresh dill

$^1/_2$ cup cider vinegar

Place the cucumbers in a large glass bowl and put the onions on top. In a small mixing bowl, combine the sugar, salt, celery seed, mustard seed, and dill. Pour in the vinegar and mix well. Pour the vinegar mixture over the cucumbers. Microwave (uncovered) on high for 3 minutes. Stir. Continue microwaving about 3 more minutes, until the onions and cucumbers are crisp-tender and the liquid is bubbly. Cover the bowl and refrigerate overnight before serving. Makes 2 to 3 servings. The recipe may be doubled.

EZ Pickled Dill Green Beans

About 1 pound fresh green beans, ends trimmed

6 sprigs fresh dill

4 cloves garlic, smashed

2 teaspoons mustard seed

1 teaspoon peppercorns

1 teaspoon salt

2 bay leaves

Dash of red pepper flakes (optional)

$2^2/_3$ cups distilled white vinegar

$2^2/_3$ cups water

2 teaspoons sugar

Place the beans upright in two 1-quart glass canning jars. Trim them to fit one-half inch below the jar's rim. Add the dill sprigs. Place the garlic, mustard seed, peppercorns, salt, bay leaves, and, if using, red pepper flakes in a large glass bowl.

In a small mixing bowl, blend the vinegar, water, and sugar. Pour over the herbs and mix well.

Microwave for 3 minutes and then stir the mixture. Return to the microwave and cook for 3 minutes more. Pour the hot liquid into the two jars equally, leaving one-half inch of headspace at the top. Screw on the lids and let cool to room temperature. After the jars have cooled, turn them upside down a couple of times to distribute the herbs more evenly. Refrigerate for 4 days before eating. These will last for a month in the fridge. Yield: 2 quarts.

Refrigerator Dill Pickles

1¹/₂ pounds small pickling cucumbers, halved lengthwise

4 fresh dill heads

4 cloves garlic, smashed

2 cups water

2 cups distilled white vinegar

1 tablespoon sugar

3 tablespoons kosher salt

1 tablespoon dill seed

¹/₂ teaspoon celery seed

1 tablespoon mustard seed

1 teaspoon red pepper flakes (optional)

Distribute the cucumbers, dill heads, and garlic evenly among four 1-pint wide-mouth canning jars.

In a large mixing bowl, blend the water, vinegar, sugar, salt, dill seed, celery seed, mustard seed, and, if using, red pepper flakes. Carefully pour an equal amount of the mixture into each jar. (It may be easier to do this with a funnel.) Add to the jar any seeds that sank to the bottom of the mixture. Screw the lids on the jars and refrigerate the pickles for 1 week before eating. Yield: 4 pints.

Pickled Carrots

1 pound carrots, peeled

1 ¹/₄ cups water

Pinch of salt

1 cup cider vinegar

¹/₄ cup sugar

2 cloves garlic, crushed slightly

1 or 2 bay leaves

1 ¹/₂ teaspoons dill seeds (may substitute fennel seeds if desired)

4 ¹/₂ teaspoons kosher salt

Cut the carrots into matchsticks slightly shorter than the height of the quart-sized jar into which you'll be putting them. Pour the water into a medium, non-aluminum saucepan and add a pinch of salt. Bring to a boil and then add the carrot sticks. Boil 1 minute *only*. Drain the carrots and rinse under cold water. Drain well, and set aside.

Put the vinegar, sugar, garlic, bay, dill (or fennel) seeds, and kosher salt into the saucepan and bring to a boil over medium heat. When the liquid boils, reduce the heat to low and simmer 2 minutes.

Remove the pan from the heat and add the carrot sticks. Let stand until carrots and liquid are at room temperature.

Pour into a clean quart-sized canning jar and refrigerate up to 4 weeks. Yield: 1 quart.

Refrigerator Bread-and-Butter Pickles

1 cup cider vinegar

³/₄ cup sugar

4 ¹/₂ teaspoons kosher salt

8 small pickling cucumbers (about one pound), unpeeled; cut into ¹/₄-inch-thick slices

1 medium onion, thinly sliced

2 teaspoons mustard seed

¹/₂ teaspoon dry mustard

¹/₂ teaspoon turmeric

¹/₄ to ¹/₂ teaspoon red pepper flakes

¹/₂ teaspoon celery seed

Place the vinegar, sugar, and salt in a large saucepan and add the cucumbers, onion, mustard seed, dry mustard, turmeric, red pepper, and celery seed. Heat to boiling over high heat, stirring occasionally. Boil 1 minute, stirring constantly.

Pour the mixture into a large bowl and cool to room temperature, stirring occasionally. Cover and chill at least 8 hours before serving, or spoon the chilled cucumbers and the liquid into sterilized canning jars with tight-fitting lids and refrigerate up to 6 weeks. Yield: About 2 quarts (or 4 pints).

Herbal Tea

Herb Garden

The earliest use of herbal teas was medicinal, but today we prize their many other benefits: subtle flavors, no caffeine, and no calories. Plus, they're inexpensive to make with herbs you've grown yourself. There's nothing more relaxing than sitting in front of a fire on a snowy winter day with your feet up and a cup of steaming lemon verbena tea warming your hands, and your insides. But herbal tea isn't just for cold weather. All of the mints make teas that are refreshing over ice—try black or white peppermint or pineapple mint. Then, have fun experimenting with various combinations of herbs—seeds, leaves, and flowers—to find flavors that appeal to the whole family.

SHOPPING LIST

Anise
Basil, cinnamon
Bergamot
Borage
Caraway
Catnip
Chamomile
Geranium, scented
Lemon balm
Lemongrass
Lemon verbena
Licorice
Mint
Rose
Rosemary
Sage, pineapple
Savory, summer or winter

The Garden

If you have a place in which to grow all the suggested herbs for teas, you'll want to arrange the plants according to their watering needs—borage, catnip, and summer savory prefer dry soil; the rest are watered regularly—and keep their mature heights in mind. Consider several beds of tea herbs, with one or two of your favorite herbs repeated in each bed.

This group includes several plants that can reach 5 feet tall or higher such as roses, lemon verbena, and lemongrass. In warm climates, pineapple sage and rosemary may reach 5 feet tall, but they aren't likely to grow that tall where they're treated as annuals. Give tall plants a home in the back of a border or in the center of beds where they can be observed from all sides. Or grow roses and lemon verbena in a spot away from the other plants.

Chamomile is a tiny edger, with winter savory topping out at a few inches taller. Anise, cinnamon basil, caraway, scented geraniums, lemon balm, and summer savory tend to grow 18 to 24 inches high. Bergamot and licorice are slightly taller, at 3 to 4 feet.

If you'd prefer to concentrate on perennial plants, these are: bergamot, catnip, chamomile, lemon balm, licorice, mints, roses, and winter savory. (Rosemary should be perennial in Zones 8 and warmer.)

All the recommended herbs, annual and perennial, will grow in containers, including roses. Mints are best grown in pots because otherwise they're generally invasive. (See page 17.) If you have only a small space, grow bergamot, chamomile, lemon balm, and mints.

Fresh or Dried?

Herbs used in tea making may be fresh or dried. Some herbs are best used fresh because they have less flavor when dried. Lemon balm is a good example. Herbs that are grown mostly for their aroma, such as many of the scented geraniums, are best when combined with stronger-flavored herbs.

Herbal Tea for a Crowd

Make an herbal tea concentrate for serving a crowd: Pour 4 cups (1 quart) boiling water over ²/₃ cup dried herbs. Cover and steep for 10 minutes. Strain into another container. Measure 2 teaspoons of the tea concentrate into a teacup and fill with boiling water. Or place 3 tablespoons in a glass and fill with ice and water. Keep extra concentrate refrigerated.

Teas made from chamomile and sweet marjoram are said to be relaxing and induce sleep. Rosemary and sage teas are considered more invigorating. Caraway, dill, lemon balm, and thyme teas have the reputation of being aids to digestion.

How to Make Herbal Tea

Pour 1 cup of boiling water over 1 rounded teaspoon dried herbs or 1 tablespoon fresh herbs and let steep for 5 minutes, then strain. (Longer steeping times can make some teas bitter.) For iced tea, generally you'll want to double the amount of herbs. To avoid straining, place the herbs in a tea ball.

Good Combinations of Herbs for Tea

- Bergamot flowers and rose petals
- Equal parts of fresh lemon balm and lemon verbena, with a sprinkling of mint
- Lemon basil and pineapple sage
- Spearmint leaves and chamomile flowers
- Orange mint, lemon balm, and anise hyssop
- Chamomile flowers and fresh lemon balm leaves
- Lemongrass and mint

Chamomile Tea

Steep 2 teaspoons dried chamomile flowers in 1 cup boiling water for 4 minutes.

Lemon-Mint Tea

2 tablespoons coarsely chopped fresh lemongrass leaves
2 tablespoons chopped fresh spearmint

Pour 2 cups boiling water over the lemongrass and mint and steep for 5 to 10 minutes. Strain and sweeten with honey if desired.

Ginger Peppermint Tea

1 cup water

2 tablespoons fresh peppermint
leaves

2 to 3 tablespoons fresh ginger
root, sliced

Bring the water to a boil and pour
over the peppermint and ginger. Let stand 4 to 5
minutes and strain. Sweeten if desired.

Summer Herbal Iced Tea Punch

$1/_4$ cup chopped fresh peppermint or spearmint

$1/_4$ cup chopped fresh lemon balm

$1/_4$ cup fresh lemon juice

$1/_4$ cup orange juice, preferably fresh

$1/_4$ cup honey, or to taste

2 liter bottle ginger ale, regular or diet, chilled

Place the mint and lemon balm in a stainless steel or heatproof
glass bowl. Combine the lemon juice, orange juice, and honey
in a small saucepan and heat until warm. Pour over the herbs.
Let stand for 1 hour. Strain. Pour the tea into a pitcher and
refrigerate if not using immediately. When ready to serve, mix in
the ginger ale. Yield: About 8 servings.

Catnip Chamomile Tea Mix

$1/_2$ cup dried catnip

$3/_4$ cup dried chamomile

$1/_4$ cup dried peppermint or spearmint

1 to $1^1/_4$ cups dried lemon balm

Fresh or frozen lemongrass, chopped (see the instructions)

Place the catnip, chamomile, mint, and lemon balm in a plastic
bowl and mix well. Cover with a lid and store in a dark place.
When you're ready to make tea, place about 2 to 3 teaspoons
of this mixture in a cup, add $1/_4$ to $1/_2$ teaspoon fresh or frozen
lemongrass, and pour boiling water over. Steep 4 to 5 minutes
and strain.

Caution: Use only the herbs recommended. Not all herbs are safe for internal consumption. Use herbal teas moderately. Some may have side effects if used excessively.

What are Rose Hips and How Do I Use Them in Teas?

Rose hips are the seedpods of rosebushes, left behind when flowers have faded. They're round and red or orange and high in Vitamin C.

Typically during summer most people prune off faded roses to encourage more flowering, so hips don't form. But many people leave the last faded flowers on a rosebush and then hips do develop. They look a bit like crabapples (the two plants are related) and are edible as long as the bush hasn't been sprayed with pesticides.

Wait until after the first hard frost to cut the hips from the bush. Not only will they taste less tart then, but that's the best time for the rosebush.

Rose hips may be used for tea when they're fresh or dried. Experiment to find the strength you like; try 4 to 7 fresh hips, mashed in the bottom of a teapot, and pour 2 cups boiling water over them. Let steep 10 minutes and strain. Or you can put 4 to 6 dried hips in 2 cups of water in a non-aluminum saucepan and bring it to a boil. Simmer 10 to 20 minutes, depending on the strength you want.

How to Dry Rose Hips

Cut hips from the bush and remove the stems, tails, and so forth. Use only unbruised and undamaged hips, without any insect holes. Wash in cool water and let dry. Slice in half and remove seeds and hairs. Place the hips in single layer on a foil- or wax paper-lined cookie sheet. Place in a dark, dry spot for about 2 weeks. Hips will dehydrate, become hard, and darken in color. You can also use a dehydrator. Store away from light in a plastic or glass container with lid. Hips may also be refrigerated or frozen.

Flowery Iced Tea

See page 33 for directions on how to make flower ice cubes to use when herbal teas are served chilled. They're "pitcher perfect" for a summertime party.

Shakespeare
Herb Garden

Dozens of plants of all types are an integral part of William Shakespeare's plays and poems—from almonds and apples to wormwood and yew. In the United States and Britain, there are a number of public Shakespeare gardens that grow a selection of these plants accompanied by a quote in which the Bard of Avon mentions it.

Any home gardener can do the same on a smaller scale. Concentrating on herbs offers a fragrant way to winnow down the huge potential selection of plants. With this herb garden project, you may find that the plays you read in school come back to you. You'll recall that rosemary is for remembrance, but did you remember that it was in *Hamlet*? And what about a rose by any other name smelling just as sweet? *Romeo and Juliet*.

SHOPPING LIST

Artemisia (wormwood)
Chamomile
Chives
Fennel
Garlic
Horseradish
Hyssop
Lavender
Lemon balm
Marjoram
Mint
Onions
Parsley
Poppy
Roses
Rosemary
Rue
Savory
Thyme
Violet

The Garden

A Shakespeare herb garden should be of a traditional design—square or rectangular with individual beds in geometric shapes laid out in a symmetrical pattern. Order and neatness were the order of the day in the "pleasaunce" (pleasure) gardens of Shakespeare's era. The entire garden would have been surrounded by a border—maybe a pleached (plaited) allee or clipped hedges of holly or boxwood, among other plants. Each bed also had a border. Here, dwarf boxwood works well, or low-growing plants such as chamomile, chives, parsley, or violets. Neat pathways throughout the garden might have been filled with sand, gravel, or tiny stepping herbs such as woolly thyme.

Topiaries of yew, privet, or rosemary were placed here and there at the intersection of paths or near seating.

Knot gardens and mazes were popular in Shakespeare's day, often created with an overlook so they could be viewed from above. Both take careful planning, planting, and almost constant care throughout the growing season.

A knot garden is designed so that the plants in it appear to be woven together in a symmetrical pattern. (Parterres, which historically are just past Shakespeare's time, are an easier version, with the plants growing together in a decorative pattern but not woven in and out.) You can outline a knot garden with an evergreen plant and then plant herbs, vegetables, or flowers inside. Or you can make the "frame" the entire knot garden. Much depends on its size.

A wormwood maze would have been a popular decorative feature. Not the sort of maze you could get lost in, since the "walls" are low-growing, but a design to enjoy viewing from a nearby sheltered bench.

Place the herbs that don't need frequent watering—lavender, rosemary, summer savory, and thyme—in the driest area. And, if you plant to include the potentially invasive plants—horseradish, mint, and wormwood—decide how you're going to control them. (See page 17 for advice.) Parsley manages well in some shade, if you have it. For the rosebush, you could go with an old-fashioned-looking David Austin rose or a more authentic Apothecary rose, which may be more difficult to locate (try online).

Some Shakespeare Gardens to Visit in the United States

Brooklyn Botanic Garden, 900 Washington Avenue, Brooklyn, NY 11225

Elizabethan Garden at the Folger Shakespeare Library, 201 East Capitol Street, SE, Washington, D.C. 20003

Elizabethan Herb Garden at Mellon Park, Fifth Avenue at Shady Avenue, Pittsburgh, PA 15206

Garden of Shakespeare's Flowers at the Golden Gate Park, Martin Luther King Jr. Drive and Middle Drive East, San Francisco, CA 94118

Shakespeare Garden, 2121 Sheridan Road, Evanston, IL 60201 (near Northwestern University)

Shakespeare Cultural Garden, Rockefeller Park, between E. 88th Street and Euclid Avenue, Cleveland, OH 44108

Shakespeare Garden at Ellis Park, 2000 Ellis Boulevard, NW, Cedar Rapids, IA 52405

Shakespeare Garden at The Huntington, 1151 Oxford Road, San Marino, CA 91108

Shakespeare Garden in Central Park, 14 E. 60th Street, New York, NY 10022

Most of the plants for this garden are perennials, but garlic, marjoram, onion, and summer savory are annuals. Rosemary may be an annual in Zones 7 and colder. Winter savory is a perennial; Shakespeare didn't specify summer or winter, so you may choose.

Fennel and roses grow about 5 feet tall and wormwood can approach that, although usually you can count on it staying about 2 to 4 feet. Rue and horseradish may reach 3 feet, but all the other plants will stay shorter.

The poppies and violets on the shopping list aren't strictly herbs, but are often included in herb gardens for their color. Although horseradish is on the list, it isn't actually mentioned by name in Shakespeare's writings. It's there because he does refer to a popular mixture of mustard and grated horseradish called Tewkesbury mustard (which is still available in Britain). Chives also aren't cited by name, but they're an *Allium*, a member of the onion family, and so many Shakespeare gardens grow them because they're perennial and onions aren't. In this case, we included them because they're considered herbs, and they surely would spoil the actors' "sweet breath" (see the quote from *A Midsummer Night's Dream.)*

Quotes from Shakespeare That Mention Herbs and Flowers

There's rosemary, that's for remembrance. Pray you, love, remember. And there is pansies, that's for thoughts . . . There's fennel for you, and columbines. There's rue for you, and here's some for me. We may call it herb of grace o' Sundays. O, you must wear your rue with a difference! There's a daisy. I would give you some violets, but they wither'd all when my father died. They say he made a good end. (HAMLET)

And, most dear actors, eat no onions nor garlic, for we are to utter sweet breath; and I do not doubt but to hear them say, it is a sweet comedy. No more words: away! go, away! (A MIDSUMMER NIGHT'S DREAM)

Here's flowers for you;
Hot lavender, mints, savoury, marjoram;
The marigold, that goes to bed wi' the sun
And with him rises weeping: these are flowers
Of middle summer, and I think they are given
To men of middle age. You're very welcome.
(THE WINTER'S TALE)

Not poppy, nor mandragora,
Nor all the drowsy syrups of the world,
Shall ever medicine thee to that
sweet sleep.
(OTHELLO)

Here did she fall a tear; here, in this place,
I'll set a bank of rue, sour herb of grace.
(KING RICHARD II)

I know a bank whereon the wild thyme blows.
(A MIDSUMMER NIGHT'S DREAM)

...so that if we will plant nettles, or sow lettuce; set hyssop...
(OTHELLO)

What's in a name? That which we call a rose
By any other name would smell as sweet.
(ROMEO AND JULIET)

For though the chamomile, the more it is trodden on, the faster
it grows, yet youth, the more it is wasted the sooner it wears.
(HENRY IV, PART 1)

Dian's bud [wormwood] o'er Cupid's flower
Hath such force and blessed power.
(A MIDSUMMER NIGHT'S DREAM)

She was the sweet marjoram of the salad.
(ALL'S WELL THAT ENDS WELL)

They are as gentle as zephyrs blowing below
the violet, not wagging his sweet head.
(CYMBELINE)

We will eat a last year's pippin [apple] of my own grafting,
with a dish of caraways, and so forth.
(KING HENRY IV, PART 2)

His wit's as thick as Tewkesbury mustard.
(HENRY IV, PART 2)

Medicinal
Herb Garden

SHOPPING LIST

Anise
Bergamot
Catnip
Chamomile
Comfrey
Dill
Fennel
Feverfew
Garlic
Germander
Horehound
Horseradish
Hyssop
Licorice
Parsley
Pot marigold
Rosemary
Sage
Thyme

Herbal medicine dates to before 2500 B.C. in China. In about 1550 B.C., an Egyptian herbal written on papyrus gave a list of plants used as drugs. Native Americans have a long history of herbal medicine, which they passed along to settlers. Through the ages, common plants—including most herbs—were thought to cure many different ailments. Science has now discovered that some of these traditional remedies were quite effective, and they've been incorporated into modern medicine. However, other old-fashioned remedies have been proven to be ineffective or, occasionally, even dangerous. Whether or not these historical remedies worked, a historic medicinal herb garden offers a fascinating peek at the past.

The Garden

Since this will be a period garden, pick an era from the past for your design (the plants were often the same from one age to another).

A medieval physic garden, for instance, would be a formal design. Monks studied the writings of the past to learn which herbs were recommended for different ailments. They then grew those herbs in a cloistered garden in small rectangular or square beds separated by narrow paths. Usually, each herb was planted in its own bed.

A more informal design was used by colonial housewives in New England, who planted gardens near their homes. These contained plants for dyeing, food, flavoring, and medical use. The effect was that of a cottage garden—a profusion of plants, some separated by narrow paths—surrounded by a fence to keep wild animals out. One interesting superstition guided the planting of a New World garden: the most fragrant plants were set apart by themselves so they wouldn't taint the soil and make the rest of the plants overly fragrant.

Several of the common healing herbs of the past—comfrey, feverfew, horseradish, and licorice—can be invasive, so you'll want to take care to control their aggressive tendencies. (See page 17.)

When you have only a small space, consider making this a container garden. Fennel and dill are too tall for containers and garlic may not mature, but all others work well. You could also limit your historic medicinal garden to two or four small squares planted with your favorites. If you have dry soil or need plants that are drought-tolerant once they're established, consider beds of anise, horehound, hyssop, rosemary, sage, and thyme. Gardeners who want to save time by planting only perennials can eliminate anise, dill, garlic, and pot marigold, which are annual, and parsley, which is biennial. Those in Zones 7 and colder can add rosemary to that list.

Chamomile, parsley, and some thymes are the natural edgers of this group of plants, with fennel and dill the tall plants in the back row or the center of a bed that's seen from all sides. Bergamot, comfrey, and feverfew may reach 4 feet, but also can stay shorter—check the label of the plants you buy to determine the variety's mature height. All the others range from 1 to 3 feet tall, depending on the cultivar, and may be placed in the middle.

The Chelsea Physic Garden

In 1673, the Chelsea Physic Garden was founded on the banks of the River Thames in London, so that apothecaries could learn to grow and know the uses of various medicinal plants. It remains an active garden today—a wonderful example of how medicinal herbs were grown in the past but also dedicated to scientific research into natural remedies, education, and conservation.

It contains the oldest cultivated rock garden in Europe and—because of its mild microclimate—many plants that normally wouldn't thrive in Britain, including a large olive tree that continues to fruit outdoors. The garden is thought to have had one of the first "glasshouses" or greenhouses in Europe, as early as 1685.

Recent additions are a garden of ethnobotany and a pharmaceutical garden, which displays plants that are used in medicine today. A Garden of World Medicine shows how people around the world have used plants as remedies. And the Historical Walk lets visitors learn the fabled history of the garden over the centuries.

The garden also works with other organizations, such as the Royal Botanic Garden at Kew and the Natural History Museum, to collect data about herbal remedies of the past.

The Chelsea Physic Garden is open to visitors Wednesdays, Thursdays, Fridays, and Sundays from April 1 through October 31. It's located at 66 Royal Hospital Road, Chelsea, London SW3 4HS. The entrance is on Swan Walk. The nearest tube station is Sloane Square.

Herbal Remedies of the Past

Anise—This was a popular herb both in Roman and Greek times, and was brought to the New World by early colonists. It was considered an all-purpose calmative (often it was given to crying babies) and was used to soothe upset stomachs.

Bergamot—The Oswego Indians drank a tea made from the dried leaves of this native plant to help relieve sore throats and colds.

Catnip—This pleasant-smelling herb was prescribed for colds and flu, insomnia, and upset stomachs.

Chamomile—Often this plant is called Roman chamomile because the ancient Romans used it for its calmative effect. (So did Peter Rabbit's mother when she made chamomile tea for Peter.)

Comfrey—This was thought to heal broken bones. (Now we know it shouldn't be taken internally.) It was also given to patients who suffered from colds.

Dill—Although associated mostly with pickles today, dill was a standby of ancient Egyptian healers. It was employed for headaches, coughs, and whooping cough, and to stimulate the appetite.

Fennel—This was the original weight-loss drug, used by ancient Greeks and Romans who needed to slim down.

Feverfew—Despite its common name, feverfew wasn't employed against fevers in the past. However, it was used from the time of ancient Rome for a wide range of ills, including headaches and colds.

Garlic—It was eaten to alleviate breathing problems, provide strength, and cure high blood pressure.

Horehound—Since at least the first century A.D., horehound has been prescribed to relieve sore throats and colds, reduce fevers, and cure malaria.

Horseradish—A wide range of ills were treated with horseradish in the past, including hay fever, poor circulation, digestive problems, congestion, coughs, stiff muscles, and rheumatism.

Hyssop—Teas made from both flowers and leaves of hyssop were used in the 1700s to treat dropsy and jaundice, and cure sore throats. A poultice of fresh hyssop leaves was said to help heal wounds and clear up black eyes.

Licorice—Licorice was used for colds, indigestion, constipation, sore throats, congestion, and ulcers, and as a laxative.

Parsley—This herb was a staple to lessen the effects of Roman orgies. Chewing parsley cleared the smell of alcohol from the breath and also helped settle the stomach. Later it was used to treat kidney and liver ailments and was employed against the plague. Parsley root was a laxative.

Pot Marigold—Not only did pot marigold produce continuous crops of colorful seasonal flowers, it was also used as a remedy for toothache, headache, heart ailments, and fever. The ancient Romans grew the plants to heal scorpion bites.

Rosemary—This fragrant herb was prescribed to stimulate the mind. Students in ancient Greece wore garlands of rosemary when studying for exams. It was burned to purify the air in sick chambers and jails. During the time of the plague, travelers tied small bags of rosemary around their necks so they could sniff it.

Sage—The Latin name for sage comes from a word meaning "to cure or save." It was prescribed for ulcers, snake bites, tuberculosis, improving memory, and stimulating the brain.

Thyme—Pillows stuffed with thyme leaves were a treatment for epilepsy at one time. Food containing large amounts of thyme were offered to cure shyness and thyme tea was supposed to alleviate nightmares. The Greeks thought that thyme was an excellent antiseptic and also prescribed it as a digestive aid.

Biblical
Herb Garden

From the fruit picked by Eve in the Garden of Eden to Jesus' parable of the mustard seed, mentions of plants abound in the Bible. The people of biblical lands were mostly agrarian and would have readily understood the references to herbs, trees, grains, and fruits, since these were part of their daily lives. Biblical gardens have grown in popularity during the past few years, fueled in part by the Internet, where it's easy to find that others have embarked on this type of garden and get firsthand advice from them. Many biblical gardens are grown around churches and synagogues, and a few have become projects of youth Sunday school classes. But some are personal gardens that combine faith and history.

SHOPPING LIST

Artemisia (wormwood)

Barley

Chamomile

Cilantro/Coriander

Cucumbers

Dill

Figs

Garlic

Grapes

Hyssop

Leeks

Lentils

Melons

Mint

Mustard

Onions

Pomegranate

Rue

Saffron

Sage

Wheat

The Garden

Even if the climate in which you live is nothing like that of the Middle East, it's certainly possible to grow a biblical garden that combines herbs with a few fruits, vegetables, and grains.

This project will give you an idea of what people ate in various Bible periods and fosters a connection to those in the past. Isn't it interesting to think of families thousands of years ago enjoying figs, grapes, melons, and pomegranates, just as your family does today? And maybe you'll wonder how home cooks long ago used sage and rue, or coriander and chamomile.

This is a garden you may want to divide into several sections. One might be planted with the biblical herbs—artemisia (wormwood), chamomile, coriander, dill, garlic, hyssop, mint, rue, saffron, and sage. If you prefer plants that return year after year, artemisia, chamomile, hyssop, mint, rue, saffron, and sage are perennials. But if this is a one-year project, such as for a class, you may prefer to stick with annuals—coriander, dill, and garlic—plus a couple of perennials, such as tricolor sage and a container of mint. When access to watering is difficult, artemisia, hyssop, and culinary sage will do fine with normal rainfall once they've become established. Saffron comes from a special crocus, a small bulb that is planted in early fall and will bloom within two or three years.

Another area of your biblical garden, or the corner of a vegetable garden, might be devoted to cucumbers, leeks, lentils, mustard, and onions. All are annuals—they produce fruit the same year they're planted and then die—except leeks, which are biennial. (Leeks flower and produce seeds their second year. Leave a few leeks in the garden to produce seeds, which you can save and plant later.) Leeks like cool, damp weather, but will do okay in warmer climates if watered regularly. In hot climates, plant them in fall for a spring harvest. Lentils need cool weather, too, and are planted several weeks before the last frost date. Harvest them in about 100 days like dried beans. Mustard is a fast-growing green that also prefers cool weather. You can plant one crop early in spring and another in fall.

The melons are the easiest fruits to grow, although they need space to roam. Figs are best in Zones 7 and warmer, although they can be grown in large containers and placed in a garage or shed over winter. Grapes require an arbor and annual pruning. Pomegranates are small trees or large shrubs that do well in Zones 8 and warmer.

Probably few home gardeners will try to grow a field of barley or wheat. But it is enjoyable to experiment with a small amount of one or both, just to see what it's like. Plant barley in late winter or early spring. Cut the stalks when they turn brittle and golden, about 50 days after sprouting. Barley spikes are especially interesting and will remind you of ornamental grasses. There are several different kinds of wheat—winter wheat, spring wheat, soft wheat, and so forth—so you'll want to get advice on the type that is best for your area, and when to plant it, from a farm store that sells wheat seed.

Biblical Passages That Mention Herbs and Other Plants

All quotes are from the King James Version.

Then shall the man bring his wife unto the priest, and he shall bring her offering for her, the tenth part of an ephah of barley meal; he shall pour no oil upon it, nor put frankincense thereon; for it is an offering of jealousy, an offering of memorial, bringing iniquity to remembrance.
(NUMBERS 5:15)

And the house of Israel called the name thereof Manna: and it was like coriander seed, white; and the taste of it was like wafers made with honey.
(EXODUS 16:31)

We remember the fish, which we did eat in Egypt freely; the cucumbers, and the melons, and the leeks, and the onions, and the garlick.
(NUMBERS 11:5)

For the fitches [dill] are not threshed with a threshing instrument, neither is a cart wheel turned about upon the cummin; but the fitches are beaten out with a staff, and the cummin with a rod.
(ISAIAH 28:27)

It's said that a rosemary plant will live no longer than Jesus did, traditionally considered to be 33 years.

He hath laid my vine waste, and barked my fig tree: he hath made it clean bare, and cast it away; the branches thereof are made white.
(JOEL 1:7)

And he fenced it, and gathered out the stones thereof, and planted it with the choicest vine, and built a tower in the midst of it, and also made a winepress therein: and he looked that it should bring forth grapes, and it brought forth wild grapes.
(ISAIAH 5:2. For a reference to grapevines, see also JOHN 15:1–8.)

And he shall take the cedar wood, and the hyssop, and the scarlet, and the living bird, and dip them in the blood of the slain bird, and in the running water, and sprinkle the house seven times.
(LEVITICUS 14:52)

And it came to pass, when David was come to Mahanaim, that Shobi the son of Nahash of Rabbah of the children of Ammon, and Machir the son of Ammiel of Lo-debar, and Barzillai the Gileadite of Rogelim, brought beds, and basons, and earthen vessels, and wheat, and barley, and flour, and parched corn, and beans, and lentiles, and parched pulse.
(2 SAMUEL 17: 27–28)

Woe unto you, scribes and Pharisees, hypocrites! for ye pay tithe of mint and anise and cummin, and have omitted the weightier matters of the law, judgment, mercy, and faith: these ought ye to have done, and not to leave the other undone.
(MATTHEW 23:23)

Another parable put he forth unto them, saying, The kingdom of heaven is like to a grain of mustard seed, which a man took, and sowed in his field: Which indeed is the least of all seeds: but when it is grown, it is the greatest among herbs, and becometh a tree, so that the birds of the air come and lodge in the branches thereof.
(MATTHEW 13:31–32)

But woe unto you, Pharisees! for ye tithe mint and rue and all manner of herbs, and pass over judgment and the love of God: these ought ye to have done, and not to leave the other undone.
(LUKE 11:42)

Some Biblical Gardens to Visit in the United States

Biblical Garden of Flowers and Herbs
    The Cathedral Church of St. John the Divine
        1047 Amsterdam Avenue, New York, NY 10025

Congregation B'nai Shalom Biblical Garden
    74 Eckley Lane, Walnut Creek, CA 94596

Edward E. Kahn Memorial Biblical Garden, Temple Sinai
    11620 Warwick Boulevard, Newport News, VA 23601

Kavanaugh UMC Biblical Garden, Kavanaugh UMC
    2516 Park Street, Greenville, TX 75401

Plants of the Bible in the Shoenberg Temperate House
    at the Missouri Botanical Garden
    4344 Shaw Boulevard, St. Louis, MO 63110

Thy plants are an orchard of pomegranates, with pleasant fruits; camphire, with spikenard, spikenard and saffron; calamus and cinnamon, with all trees of frankincense; myrrh and aloes, with all the chief spices: A fountain of gardens, a well of living waters, and streams from Lebanon.
(SONG OF SOLOMON 4:13–15)

Lest there should be among you man, or woman, or family, or tribe, whose heart turneth away this day from the LORD our God, to go and serve the gods of these nations; lest there should be among you a root that beareth gall and wormwood.
(DEUTERONOMY 29:18)

But the wheat and the rie were not smitten: for they were not grown up.
(EXODUS 9:32)

So she kept fast by the maidens of Boaz to glean unto the end of barley harvest and of wheat harvest; and dwelt with her mother in law.
(RUTH 2:23)

Herbs are among the easiest plants you can grow. Most prefer sun but will live happily in partial shade, and many require little watering. Here's a look at the basics of growing herbs.

Soil

The best soil for an herb garden would be similar to what's in a vegetable garden. But for most herbs, "ordinary" soil—where weeds, grass, or other plants grow well—is fine. Some herbs require "rich" soil, which has been improved with or already contains quite a bit of organic matter. A few perform best in poor soil, those dry spots where little else will live. The plant profiles on the following pages will tell you which herbs have preferences for one or the other.

Drainage

When choosing a place for your herbs, keep drainage in mind. Although some herbs prefer moist soil, that doesn't mean soil that stays wet all the time. In most cases, nothing will kill herbs faster than soil that doesn't drain well—and that's especially true of a garden spot that remains wet during winter. In poorly drained soil, roots stay too wet and are deprived of oxygen, causing them to rot and the plant to die.

Light

All plants need light to grow. Those described as requiring "full sun" in the following pages need 7 or more hours of direct sun each day. Herbs that can manage in partial shade should receive 5 hours of direct sun and some dappled light the rest of the day. Often gardeners in hot climates find that some herbs that like full sun in moderate climates are more successful in the heat if given a little afternoon shade to protect them. If your herb garden doesn't have full sun in all areas, try some of the plants marked "partial shade" to see which perform best for you in different spots. Just remember that having enough sunlight matters. An herb garden isn't a shade garden.

Water

Gardeners generally think of herbs as thrifty with water. Mature herbs native to Mediterranean hillsides require little water. Others need added moisture in dry spells and droughts. But many herbs need regular watering, just like tomato or petunia plants.

The profiles let you know which herbs require extra moisture whenever rainfall is less than an inch a week, but here are some general guidelines:

Young plants need watering more frequently than older, more established plants because their roots haven't had time to become established.

Annuals need more frequent watering than perennials that are 2 or more years old.

Plants in containers need regular watering, because their soil dries faster than soil in a garden. Clay pots dry out sooner than plastic ones.

Plants in hot climates need more water than those in more moderate temperatures.

Mulched plants need less water than those that are not mulched.

Fertilizer

If the soil in your herb garden contains plenty of organic matter, you may never need to fertilize herb plants, except to get new ones off to a good start. But if your soil is deficient in nutrients and you're growing annual herbs or others that need richer soil, fertilize lightly several times during the season (in late spring and early summer, for instance). An advantage of organic fertilizers is that they feed plants slowly throughout the growing season. If you use a water-soluble plant food, mix it at half strength. Herbs that receive too much fertilizer have weak stems that easily fall over and break, and the plants generally don't have a strong flavor.

Pests

It's true that herbs may be bothered less by pests than other types of plants. But that doesn't mean they have no pest problems. At different times aphids, spider mites, scale, or slugs may decide that your herbs would make a great meal. Insecticidal soap—available at garden centers—can help control all but slugs. (For them, try saucers of beer or yeast dissolved in water. The slugs are attracted to the yeast and drown.) But you may also find that a strong stream of water directed at both sides of the leaves of plants attacked by aphids or spider mites will take care of the problem. And you can scrape scale off stems when the insects are young. If other insect or disease problems crop up, check with your local agricultural Cooperative Extension office for an organic control.

Anise was one of the first herbs planted in colonial American gardens.

Anise

Pimpinella anisum

Annual

Height: Up to 2 feet

Anise, which has a mild licorice flavor, is grown mostly for its seeds. Because the seeds take 4 months to form and ripen, anise does best in areas with a long growing season. In cooler climates, the plant can be grown for its leaves, which taste like the seeds.

Getting Started: In spring, after frost has passed and soil has warmed, sow seeds outdoors in ordinary, well-drained soil and full sun. Space 15 inches apart. In the Deep South, anise is usually a fall-planted crop that blooms in spring.

Growing: Water during dry spells. Fertilize only if soil is very poor.

Harvesting & Uses: Snip off small amounts of leaves as needed and flowers for fresh use just as they open. The seeds start to ripen about 4 weeks after flowering. Cut the flower stalk at the base and place in a large paper bag with holes punched in the sides for air circulation. Hang the bags in a cool, dry place. Or hang stalks upside down over newspaper. Seeds remain good for 3 years. Use seeds in baked goods and potpourri; use fresh leaves and flowers in salads.

Recommended Varieties: No cultivars are readily available.

Anise hyssop, which self-sows, has been known to grow in the cracks of sidewalks. Native Americans used it as a sweetener.

Anise hyssop

Agastache foeniculum

Perennial to Zone 4

Height: Up to 4 feet

If you're looking for a butterfly magnet that's very easy to grow, anise hyssop is it. This native prairie wildflower also attracts bees and hummingbirds to your garden. It's useful in cooking and in making potpourri.

Getting Started: Sow seeds indoors about 6 weeks before the last frost date in spring, or outdoors after all danger of frost has passed. Place plants or seeds 12 inches apart in fertile, well-drained soil and full sun to partial shade.

Growing: Anise hyssop is drought tolerant once it's established, but you may need to water during dry spells when the plant is young. Fertilize once or twice during the growing season if it seems to need a boost. After the first flush of flowers, cut back to encourage rebloom and to discourage rampant self-sowing.

Harvesting & Uses: Cut leaves as needed for fresh use; they will be more flavorful before the plant flowers. Pick flowers just as they open. Preserve by drying. Use in teas and potpourri.

Recommended Varieties: 'Tutti Fruti' has raspberry blooms; 'Snow Spike' has white flowers. 'Fragrant Delight' is perennial only in Zones 8–11.

Wormwood (Artemisia absinthium) is one of the bitterest herbs known. Hung near a home's door, it was supposed to prevent visits by witches and goblins. Wormwood was strewn on the floor to repel fleas.

Artemisia

Artemisia spp. and hybrids

Perennial (zones vary)

Height: 2 to 5 feet

Artemisias have gray or silver foliage and all prefer to be kept on the dry side. The species vary in size and in zones in which they do best. All are popular for their landscaping value as well as for their contribution to craft projects.

Getting Started: Set out plants in spring after weather is warm, spacing 2 to 4 feet apart in ordinary, well-drained soil and full sun. They also grow in containers.

Growing: Trim plants the second and following springs to shape them. Dig out any that have spread by runners. (Artemisia may be invasive in some parts of the country.)

Harvesting & Uses: Pick leaves as needed and dry them. Use leaves in crafts. Use plants in landscaping and night gardens.

Recommended Varieties: Southernwood (*Artemisia abrotanum*) has soft foliage and grows 3 to 5 feet tall in Zones 6 and warmer. *A. absinthium* 'Silver King' and *A. absinthium* 'Silver Queen' are excellent cultivars of wormwood, growing 2 to 3 feet high and performing better than most in the humid South (perennial to Zone 5). Sweet Annie (*A. annua*) is a 5-foot annual usually grown for wreath-making.

To impart extra flavor to a roasted chicken, tuck several bay leaves into the cavity of the bird before putting it in the oven. Remove before serving.

Bay

Laurus nobilis

Perennial to Zone 8

Height: Up to 50 feet in the garden

Bay is actually an evergreen tree and, in the right conditions, a big one, but in cold-winter climates, it can be grown in a large pot, outdoors in summer and indoors in cold weather. It's a slow grower.

Getting Started: Plant a young tree in rich, well-drained soil in full sun or partial shade. (In hot climates, bay needs a bit of afternoon shade). In cold-winter climates, grow in a large container. In Zone 7, buy a tree that's hardy to 0 degrees F and put it in a spot that's protected from winter winds.

Growing: Fertilize in spring. Water container plants regularly. Pinch the tips of the stems to make the plant bushier. Indoors, apply rubbing alcohol if scale or mealybugs appear. Outdoors, spray scale with horticultural oil. In climates where hardiness is marginal, mulch heavily in fall.

Harvesting & Uses: Pick leaves as needed and dry them for later use. A flower press will make them dry flat. Use leaves in cooking, wreaths, and potpourri, and on coals when grilling; use plants in biblical gardens.

Recommended Varieties: 'Angustifolia' has leaves with wavy edges.

Basil

Ocimum spp.

Annual

Height: Up to 2 to 2 ¹/₂ feet

Over the past few decades, Americans have gone bonkers for basil. It's now the herb we eat the most of, pushing parsley out of the number-one spot. (This seems especially apt because the Greek word from which we derive the word basil means "king.") With this burgeoning popularity—or maybe contributing to it—has come an explosion in the number of basils available to home gardeners. With dozens available, how do you choose? You'll want to have fun experimenting, but see our recommendations below.

Getting Started: Basil likes heat, so there's no point in trying to rush it in the spring. Wait to sow seeds or set out plants until soil and air temperatures are both warm. Space 12 to 18 inches apart in full sun and rich, moist but well-drained soil. Basil grows well in containers.

Growing: Basil will perform best in hot summers. Fertilize monthly during the growing season. Water regularly, as you would tomato plants. Cut off the first flowers that develop so the plants will produce more leaves and become bushier. The first light frost of fall will kill the plants, so make sure you've harvested all you need before that.

Harvesting & Uses: Cut basil leaves as needed and the flowers as they open. Leaves will be more flavorful before the plant has bloomed. Never refrigerate basil—it turns black. Cut stems of basil and place in a vase or jar of water to use as needed. (Basil stays fresh for a couple of weeks.) Traditional methods of drying herbs don't work well with basil, which either blackens or loses its flavor. One preservation method is to blend the leaves with olive or vegetable oil and refrigerate or freeze in small quantities. (Purée 1 cup basil leaves in a food processor or blender and mix in 1 to 2 tablespoons oil. Freeze in ice cube trays or in dollops on a cookie sheet. Transfer to a plastic bag once they're frozen.) Use basil in pestos, teas, cooking, baking, vinegars, and flavored oils.

Recommended Varieties: Sweet basil (*O. basilicum*) has the familiar basil flavor and large leaves. One of the best-flavored sweet basils for cooking is 'Genoa Sweet'. 'Green Ruffles' has a spicy taste you might like. *O. basilicum* var. *purpurascens* 'Purple Ruffles' is one of the most reliable of the purple-leaf basils. *O. tenuiflorum* (formerly *O. sanctum*) is holy basil, which has a wonderful scent. Thai basil (*O. basilicum* 'Horopha') has the flavor and scent of anise. Lettuce-leaf basil has big, crinkly leaves. Lemon basil (*O.* x *citriodorum*) has the sharp lemon flavor of other lemony herbs. Cinnamon basil (*O. basilicum* 'Cinnamon') really does smell like cinnamon. A good bush basil is 'Spicy Globe'.

Chew on fresh leaves of basil or parsley to eliminate the odor of garlic on your breath.

After the Boston Tea Party, the early American colonists used bergamot to brew tea. This tea was introduced to them by the Oswego Indians.

Bergamot

Monarda didyma

Perennial to Zone 4

Height: Up to 4 feet

Bergamot has many names—monarda, bee balm, and bergamot—but "bergamot" is the one most likely to be used by herbalists. It's a flamboyant native plant whose colorful, scented flowers are quite an attraction for bees, butterflies, and hummingbirds. (People like the leaves' orange flavor too.)

Getting Started: Choose mildew-resistant cultivars and set out plants 2 feet apart in spring after danger of frost is past. Provide rich, moist soil and full sun or partial shade. Bergamot is an excellent container plant and growing it in pots prevents its spread.

Growing: Keep soil evenly moist. Fertilize in spring. Deadhead to encourage more blooming. Remove mildewed leaves. Watch out for slugs. Remove unwanted plants. (It can be mildly invasive.)

Harvesting & Uses: For drying, pick leaves before the plant flowers so they'll have the strongest flavor. Cut flowers just as they open and use fresh or dry. Use in cooking, teas, wreaths, potpourri, and for fragrance.

Recommended Varieties: Relatively mildew resistant are 'Marshall's Delight', 'Petite Wonder', and 'Jacob Cline'.

For an attractive color combination, plant borage next to rue.

Borage

Borago officinalis

Annual

Height: Up to 2¹/₂ feet

Folklore says that eating cucmber-flavored borage will give you courage. Probably not, but it does contain high levels of potassium.

Getting Started: After chance of frost has passed, sow seed outdoors in moist but well-drained soil. (Because it has a deep taproot, borage doesn't transplant well.) It prefers a location in full sun, but tolerates part shade. If possible, plant on a slight rise, to better enjoy the flowers. If you want to grow borage in a container, choose a pot that's a couple of feet wide. Consider planting borage near tomatoes or strawberries since it attracts bees for pollination.

Growing: In the Deep South and in frost-free climates, gardeners may want to grow borage as a cool-season plant. In hot weather, keep the plant well watered. Remove faded flowers to encourage longer blooming. When plants have been killed by frost, dispose of them away from the garden; in the compost pile, seeds often germinate later.

Harvesting & Uses: Pick leaves to use fresh. Its taste is best before the plant flowers. Pick flowers as they fully open. Both leaves and flowers may be dried. Use borage in vinegars, potpourri, crystallized flowers, as fresh flowers, and in cooking.

Recommended Varieties: 'Alba' has white flowers.

Evidence of caraway's use in cooking dates back at least 5,000 years. All of the plant's parts are edible.

Caraway

Carum carvi

Biennial

Height: 18 to 24 inches

Caraway is grown mostly for its seeds, which are used in rye bread and tea, and seasoning vegetables such as cabbage. The carrotlike leaves may be added to soups and salads.

Getting Started: Caraway doesn't like heat and humidity, but can tolerate temperatures into the mid-20s F; plant in fall in Zones 8 and warmer. Elsewhere, sow seeds in the garden where they will grow in early spring. (Caraway doesn't transplant well.) Give the plants full sun in cool climates, a bit of afternoon shade where it's warmer. Soil should be rich with good drainage. Space 8 inches apart. Caraway is not a good choice for containers.

Growing: During the growing season, water when rainfall is less than an inch per week. Fertilize the plants when they flower. Mulch over winter.

Harvesting & Uses: As a biennial, caraway flowers its second summer after planting. Cut the flowers when they turn brown. Hang stems upside-down from rafters. Surround them with a paper bag that has holes cut in the sides for air circulation and the seeds will fall into the bag when they're dry. Use seeds in cooking, baking, teas, and potpourri.

Recommended Varieties: No cultivars are readily available.

Catnip is a member of the mint family. It's said to deter flea beetles when planted next to vegetables.

Catnip

Nepeta cataria

Perennial to Zone 4

Height: 2 to 3 feet

While catnip is sure to be of interest to cat lovers, it's also a good herb for tea, and its flowers are edible.

Getting Started: In spring, sow seeds indoors or outdoors, or set out plants into the garden 12 to 18 inches apart. Grow in full sun or partial shade and light, well-drained soil. Seeds are slow to germinate. Catnip can grow in containers. If felines roll against the plant and cause problems, put a wire cage around it, or plant it in a spot that's inaccessible to cats. Keep catnip away from other plants cats could damage.

Growing: Catnip is drought resistant, so watering isn't often needed. Cut the plant back hard when it begins to bloom, so it will produce more leaves. Remove flowers just as they fade to avoid self-sowing.

Harvesting & Uses: Pick flowers just as they open for fresh use or drying. Young leaves are best for tea. Dry leaves and flowers by hanging or on a screen. Use dried leaves in teas and as stuffing for cat toys; use fresh leaves or flowers in salads.

Recommended Varieties: Try lemon catnip, *Nepeta cataria* 'Citriodora'.

To make blond hair appear even fairer, use a chamomile rinse. (Add 1 ounce of dried chamomile or 2 ounces of fresh to 2 cups of water in a saucepan. Bring to a boil, reduce heat, cook for 10 minutes, then let stand until cool. Strain.)

Chamomile

Chamaemelum nobile

Perennial to Zone 4 (may be an annual in the hot and humid South)

Height: 10 inches

Gardeners know that Peter Rabbit's mom was on to a good thing when she gave her little adventurer a cup of chamomile tea to calm him down before bed. The herb is often called Roman chamomile. German chamomile (*Matricaria recutia*) and other "false" chamomiles are in different genuses.

Getting Started: In spring, start seeds indoors 6 weeks before last frost, or sow seeds in ordinary, well-drained soil in full sun or partial shade after chance of frost has passed. May also sow seeds in fall, especially in the South. Space plants 12 to 16 inches apart. Can be grown between stones in a path and in containers.

Growing: Keep soil moist during the growing season. Pull up unwanted self-sown plants.

Harvesting & Uses: Chamomile's lacy foliage is fragrant, but the tiny, daisylike flowers produce the apple-scented tea. Harvest leaves as needed. Pick flowers as they open. Dry flowers on a screen or hang them up. Use in teas and potpourri.

Recommended Varieties: 'Flore Pleno' has strong-scented double flowers.

Candy made from the roots of chervil was thought to prevent the plague.

Chervil

Anthriscus cerefolium

Annual

Height: 1 to 2 feet

Anyone who enjoys cooking will want to grow chervil, an ingredient in traditional *fines herbes* as well as part of a bouquet garni.

Getting Started: In spring when the weather is still cool, sow seeds outdoors in rich, moisture-retentive soil. (Chervil doesn't transplant well.) In Zones 8 and warmer, sow seeds in fall. The plants prefer full sun in cool climates, but tolerate partial shade. Sow seeds at 3-week intervals through spring to prolong the harvest. Chervil grows in containers in partial shade, in a window box, or indoors on a bright windowsill.

Growing: Fertilize twice during the growing season. Water at least once a week. To prolong the harvest, clip off flower stalks as they develop to keep the plant from going to seed since the herb's flavor is best before the plant has flowered.

Harvesting & Uses: Dried leaves don't have much flavor; it's better to freeze them. Use in French cooking, seasoning mixes, and grilling.

Recommended Varieties: 'Crispum' has curly leaves but not as much flavor as other members of the species. It's pretty as a garnish. 'Brussels Winter' grows 2 feet tall and is slow to go to seed.

The old English saying, "Chives next to roses creates posies" comes from the practice of planting chives near rosebushes to deter blackspot disease.

Chives

Allium schoenoprasum

Perennial to Zone 4

Height: 12 to 18 inches

If you have space or time for only a couple of herbs, choose chives as one of them. It's easy to grow, has perky little flowers, and is one of the most useful herbs in the kitchen.

Getting Started: Sow seeds indoors or outside in early spring. Or set plants about 6 inches apart in full sun and rich, moist soil.

Growing: Water as you would tomatoes. Fertilize twice during the growing season. Divide every 3 years in fall. Harvest regularly.

Harvesting & Uses: Pick flowers as they open. Cut stalks at the base anytime they're green. You can also trim the entire plant back to 4 inches high and let it renew itself. Freeze stalks for later use. Use chives in cooking, salads, garnish, marinades, as fresh flowers, and dried flowers in crafts.

Recommended Varieties: 'Grolau' does well indoors and in greenhouses. Garlic chives (or Chinese chives), *A. tuberosum*, has flat leaves rather than hollow, white flowers, and a garlicky flavor. It can be aggressive. *Tulbaghia violacea*, society garlic, is similar to garlic chives, but grows especially well in hot, humid climates. *T. violacea* 'Tricolor' has pink, green, and white leaves.

Cilantro/coriander is one of the oldest herbs to be cultivated. It's known to have been grown at least since the Bronze Age.

Cilantro/Coriander

Coriandrum sativum

Annual

Height: 1 to 3 feet

Cilantro and coriander are the same plant—the leaves are called cilantro, while the seeds are known as coriander. So gardeners get two plants in one with this easy annual.

Getting Started: Sow seeds in early spring. Space 6 to 9 inches apart in full sun or partial shade and ordinary soil. (Cilantro doesn't transplant well.) Sow more seeds at 3-week intervals to prolong the harvest. In Zones 8 and warmer, plant in fall.

Growing: Don't allow the soil to dry out; water regularly and mulch. Keep the bed weeded. Remove unwanted self-sown plants.

Harvesting & Uses: Cut lower leaves for fresh use. Preserve in olive oil or freeze in ice cube trays. Remove seedpods when they turn brown and develop a pleasant scent. Dry by hanging plant stalks upside-down inside a paper bag to collect seeds as they fall. When seeds are dry, rub them between your hands to remove the seed coat. Store in the refrigerator. Use both in Mexican and Asian cooking, potpourri, vinegars, and marinades.

Recommended Varieties: Slow-bolting cultivars are 'Slow Bolt' and 'Longstanding'. (Bolting refers to going to seed rapidly, usually in response to hot weather.) 'Morocco' is good in warmer regions.

Comfrey is best for external uses. Studies have reported it to be a suspected carcinogen when taken internally.

Comfrey

Symphytum officinale

Perennial

Height: 10 inches to 4 feet

Comfrey brings two advantages to the herb garden—it blooms a long time and bees love it. But it has one huge disadvantage—it spreads rapidly and should be treated as invasive.

Getting Started: Place plants outdoors after danger of frost has passed. Space them 3¹/₂ feet apart in full sun or partial shade and rich, moist soil. It's a good choice for containers that are kept off the ground (watch out for roots escaping through the drainage hole).

Growing: Fertilize two or three times during the growing season. If the plant gets weedy looking, cut it back to 4 inches high and let it regrow. Take cuttings in summer, if desired. In fall, add the spent plants to the compost pile or use them as mulch.

Harvesting & Uses: Cut leaves when they're young, before they become hairy. Spread them on a screen, not touching, to dry. Dried leaves have cosmetic uses; yellow dye can be made from fresh leaves.

Recommended Varieties: Dwarf comfrey (*S. grandiflorum*) is a compact plant with blue flowers that are slightly larger than other species.

In the Middle Ages, magicians used dill in spells to protect against witches. The word "dill" may have come from a Norse word meaning "calm." It was often used to calm upset stomachs.

Dill

Anethum graveolens

Annual

Height: $1^1/_2$ to 5 feet

Without dill, we wouldn't have dill pickles, but this herb's uses extend beyond that—its flowers are used fresh and dried, and its leaves flavor many types of cooking.

Getting Started: In early spring (or fall in mild climates), sow seeds 12 to 18 inches apart outdoors. (Dill doesn't transplant well.) Place in full sun and in good, moist soil in an area that is protected from strong winds. The seeds need light to germinate, so cover very lightly. In containers, dill may need staking.

Growing: Water regularly. Fertilize when flowering begins. Remove flowers to encourage foliage growth. Dill is the host plant for the larvae of the swallowtail butterfly, so plant enough both for you and them.

Harvesting & Uses: Begin harvesting leaves when the plant is 12 inches high. Use quickly, leaves last only a day refrigerated. They don't dry well. Harvest seeds when they begin to turn brown and dry or freeze them. Use leaves and seeds in cooking, pickling, and vinegars.

Recommended Varieties: 'Tetra' and 'Dukat' are slow to bolt (go to seed). 'Fernleaf' grows only 18 inches high and is good for containers and flower beds.

Fennel leaves may be added to many dishes— fish, eggs, vegetables— near the end of cooking. Fresh stems flavor salads and soups, while fennel seeds are used in sausage, sauerkraut, potato dishes, and breads.

Fennel

Foeniculum vulgare

Perennial to Zone 5

Height: 5 to 6 feet or taller

Isn't fennel a vegetable? There are two types of fennel, and one, Florence fennel, is indeed grown as a vegetable. But *Foeniculum vulgare*, known as sweet fennel, definitely belongs in your herb garden and in your kitchen. Its lovely feathery foliage and cheery yellow flowers are an asset to the landscape, and its anise flavor will brighten many a meal.

Getting Started: Sow seeds directly in the garden in spring, once soil has reached about 60 degrees F. Sweet fennel likes a sunny site with well-drained soil. Place it so it doesn't shade smaller, sun-loving plants. Space about 20 inches apart. It's not a good container plant because of its height.

Growing: Mulch to keep soil moist and water during dry spells. Pull up unwanted self-sown plants.

Harvesting & Uses: Cut leaves for fresh use before the plant flowers. They don't dry well but may be frozen. Cut blooms as they open. Harvest seeds after they dry and turn brown but before they fall. Use in cooking, baking, and salads, and as edible flowers.

Recommended Varieties: 'Bronze' and 'Rubrum' have bronze-red foliage.

Because the odor of feverfew is said to repel bees, it's usually not planted near plants, such as tomatoes, that need bees for pollination.

Feverfew

Tanacetum parthenium

Perennial to Zone 5

Height: 1 to 4 feet

Feverfew has been useful since the days of ancient Rome. It's also an attractive garden plant, with small daisylike flowers that appear in midsummer. Where winters are mild, it's evergreen. Because it self-sows prolifically, it may be invasive.

Getting Started: Sow seeds indoors or in the garden in spring after the last frost date. Place 12 inches apart in full sun to partial shade in average, well-drained soil. (Feverfew also grows in poor, rocky soil.) Good drainage is essential. It's a good choice for containers, since they halt the plants' spread.

Growing: Mulch plants lightly to discourage self-sowing. Water is needed only during drought. Remove unwanted self-sown plants (they pull up easily). Remove faded flowers promptly. Shear back the plant after the first flowers fade to encourage reblooming.

Harvesting & Uses: Cut flowers just after they've opened and use them fresh or dried. Pick leaves before the plant blooms. Freeze them. Use for fresh flowers, in potpourri and crafts, and as a dye.

Recommended Varieties: 'Aureum' has gold leaves; 'White Stars' has double flowers.

Geranium, scented

Pelargonium spp. and hybrids

Annual except in Zones 10 and 11

Height: 1$^1/_2$ to 3 feet

You'll want to buy scented geraniums in person so you can touch the leaves and sniff out which fragrances you like best and which live up to their names. They're an intriguing group of plants, with leaf scents that range from lemon and rose to chocolate and apple and include peppermint and strawberry. It's easy to see why they're treasured for potpourri and sachets, as well as many other uses. The leaves of scented geraniums also appeal to the other senses—they may resemble small oak leaves or ornate ferns and often they feel just like velvet. Scented geraniums come in two sizes—smaller plants with small leaves and larger plants with bigger leaves. Space them accordingly, although they generally spread more than the gardener expects them to.

Rose and lemon are the most popular fragrances of scented geraniums. Thomas Jefferson brought several scented geraniums to the White House when he became president.

Getting Started: In spring, after the danger of frost has passed, set out plants in rich, well-drained soil and full sun to partial shade. Scented geraniums grow well in containers and can be trained as standards. (A plant grown with a single, strong center stem that is its main support is said to be a "standard" form.)

Growing: Water regularly and fertilize monthly. Pinch the plant regularly to encourage branching and to keep the plant shaped. If aphids or whiteflies appear, spray with insecticidal soap. Remove flowers as they fade so the seedpods don't ripen and sow seeds all over the area.

Harvesting & Uses: Pick leaves as desired throughout the growing season. They will be more fragrant before the plant has bloomed. Cut flowers, which are edible, as they open. Use fresh or dry them. Use in cooking, baking, vinegars, potpourri, sachets, and nosegays.

Recommended Varieties: *Pelargonium quercifolium*, oak-leaf geranium, has variegated leaves and a spicy scent. *P.* 'Lemon Fancy' is one of the strongest scented of the lemon geraniums. *P.* 'Mabel Grey' is almost as strong and has diamond-shaped leaves. The foliage of *P.* 'Chocolate Peppermint' smells just as you would expect it to. *P.* x *fragans* has a nutmeg scent. *P. graveolens* 'Tomentosa' has furry foliage with a peppermint fragrance, a winning combination. *P. crispum* 'Peach Cream' produces cream and gold variegated leaves that are crinkled and have a nice peach scent. *P. graveolens* 'Silver Rose' combines silver leaves and a nice rose fragrance. Also look for cultivars with rose, lime, ginger, strawberry, apple, and other scents. You'll be amazed at what you'll find.

Garlic was long considered a magical herb, widely used in spells to ward off evil. Ancient herbalists were writing about its supposed medicinal properties 4,000 years ago.

Garlic

Allium sativum

Usually grown as an annual.

Height: 18 to 24 inches

Garlic is essential in the kitchen, and many people use it medicinally. It may also deter pests in the garden.

Getting Started: In fall, pull cloves from a garlic bulb and plant the largest ones, pointed end up, 4 to 6 inches apart and 2 inches deep, in full sun and moist, well-drained soil. Garlic does fine in containers.

Growing: Provide an inch of water per week and fertilize twice in spring. Remove flower stalks to promote bigger bulbs. Mulch during winter in cold climates.

Harvesting & Uses: Cut green leaves for fresh use. When the tops yellow and fall over, dig up the bulbs. Dry them on a screen or hang in an airy, shaded place. When its covering is paperlike (about 3 weeks), remove tops and roots, leaving an inch of stem. Store in a cool, dry place; don't refrigerate. Alternatively, separate the cloves and keep them in the freezer. Or drop peeled cloves into a jar of olive oil and refrigerate. Use in cooking, for decorative and medicinal purposes, and in insect spray.

Recommended Varieties: 'Early Red Italian', 'Persian Star', and 'Spanish Roja'. For warm climates, try elephant garlic (*Allium ampeloprasum*).

Horehound has been soothing sore throats since the time of the ancient Greeks.

Horehound

Marrubium vulgare

Perennial to Zone 4

Height: 1 1/2 to 3 feet

Horehound is best known for soothing sore throats, but its downy gray leaves and white flowers make it visible in the garden after dark. It also attracts butterflies and bees.

Getting Started: In spring, sow seeds indoors or outdoors. Space seedlings 12 to 14 inches apart in full sun. Horehound tolerates dry, poor soil, but it prefers sandy, well-drained soil. It does fine in containers.

Growing: In summer, remove flowers to prevent self-sowing and pull up unwanted self-sown plants. Horehound tolerates heat and drought, so it rarely needs watering. In winter, it may rot if drainage is poor. In the second and succeeding years, cut back plants in spring to make them bushier. (You may also prune the plant after flowering.) In spring, divide plants if desired, but you may not need to since they are prolific self-seeders.

Harvesting & Uses: Pick leaves from the top half of the plant just before it blooms. Dry and store in a zipper-type plastic bag. Use the plant as an ornamental in night gardens, and to attract butterflies and bees. The leaves are used for medicinal purposes.

Recommended Varieties: 'Green Pompon' is a good one.

The "horse" part of the common name indicates that this is a large or coarse plant. When cooked, horseradish's strong flavor tends to dissipate quickly.

Horseradish

Armoracia rusticana

Perennial to Zone 3

Height: Up to 3 feet

Horseradish, grown for its pungent root, tolerates almost any garden conditions and thrives on neglect. It can be invasive, though.

Getting Started: In spring, plant small root cuttings in full sun and average soil, although they will grow just about anywhere. Dig 12 inches deep to loosen the soil and plant about 12 inches apart.

Growing: Mulch plants to prevent weeds.

Harvesting & Uses: Except in climates with very long growing seasons, harvesting begins the second year. Loosen soil carefully, remove brittle side shoots, and dig out roots. (Beware: Any piece of root left in the ground will produce new plants.) Cut off the top and remaining side shoots and wash the root. Place in a perforated mesh bag (such as onions come in) and store in the refrigerator for up to 3 months. To use, grate a month's supply and store in the refrigerator. (To lessen fumes, grate in a food processor.) In warm climates, horseradish can be left in the ground over winter under mulch and dug up as needed. Use in cooking and for medicinal purposes.

Recommended Varieties: 'Maliner Kren' has large roots and excellent flavor.

In the days before spray cans of air freshener, imagine that you have a musty castle. How to make it smell more pleasant? Strew dried hyssop around the rooms. That's what they did long ago.

Hyssop

Hyssopus officinalis

Perennial to Zone 4

Height: $1^1/_2$ to $2^1/_2$ feet

Long-blooming hyssop brightens the herb garden from summer into fall. You'll find decorative plants with edible blue, pink, or white flowers that are great in salads. The plant is evergreen in mild climates.

Getting Started: In spring, sow seeds indoors or buy plants. Hyssop prefers full sun and will grow in ordinary, well-drained soil. This is a good plant for a dry spot. Space 2 feet apart. Hyssop also grows in large containers.

Growing: Hyssop is drought tolerant so it usually needs little watering. After their first year, cut back plants in spring to make them more compact. Propagate by division or cuttings.

Harvesting & Uses: Cut flowers for fresh use when they're almost open. Pick leaves as needed. (They'll have a stronger flavor before the plant flowers.) Dry leaves and flowers to preserve them. Use both leaves and flowers for culinary purposes and potpourri. Use plants for fragrance and to attract butterflies, and as an attractive edging or short hedge in the herb garden; they can be clipped for a knot garden.

Recommended Varieties: Try 'Rubra' and 'Aristata' (a dwarf cultivar good for edging).

If you don't care for the spring flowers of lamb's ears, try 'Silver Carpet', which doesn't bloom. 'Big Ears' is for those who want even larger leaves for wreaths and craft projects.

Lamb's ears

Stachys byzantina

Perennial to Zone 5

Height: Up to 18 inches

Whether you consider lamb's ears a perennial flower or an herb, it's a charming addition to an herb garden. And who can pass one without stopping to rub the "furry" ear-shaped leaves? But it isn't a good choice for areas with high humidity and may rot in hot, rainy summers.

Getting Started: Start with seeds sown indoors or plants outdoors. Grow in full sun or part shade in average, well-drained soil. Space 12 to 18 inches apart.

Growing: Water during dry spells, but avoid overwatering when rainfall amounts are normal. Slugs and snails may be a problem. Remove damaged leaves to improve the plant's appearance. Some gardeners like to remove the insignificant flowers too. In early spring, cut the semi-evergreen plant back to encourage better regrowth. Divide in spring or fall.

Harvesting & Uses: Cut fresh leaves to use in flower arrangements. Dry for use in craft projects. Use plants in a night garden, a garden of all-white plants, or a rock garden, and in borders. It's a fun plant for youngsters, who love to touch the leaves.

Recommended Varieties: Try 'Silver Carpet' or 'Big Ears'.

Lavender is now grown throughout the world. In ancient Greece and Rome, it was added to bathwater, and its name comes from the Latin word lavare, *which means "to wash."*

Lavender

Lavandula spp. and hybrids

Perennial to Zone 5

Height: 1¹/₂ to 3 feet

Lavender is such a romantic plant—both in its evocative fragrance and its appearance. Just one whiff and you'll feel relaxed. And what gardener wouldn't love to recreate fields of lavender like those in France?

Getting Started: Lavender is more difficult to grow in humid climates—choose the right cultivars. In all climates, full sun and excellent drainage are essential; soil should be slightly alkaline. Start with purchased plants. If you don't have ideal conditions, grow lavender in containers filled with cactus potting mix.

Growing: Water during dry spells. Remove faded flowers. In spring, prune out dead wood and lightly shape the plant. Propagate by cuttings in spring.

Harvesting & Uses: In midafternoon, cut flowers as the buds begin to open. Use fresh or dried flowers in cooking; use dried flowers in sachets and potpourri. Use plants to attract butterflies and for fragrance; they work well in an evening or rock garden.

Recommended Varieties: 'Hidcote' is good for drying. 'Munstead' grows in many climates. *Lavandula* x *intermedia* cultivars tolerate high humidity.

Lemon balm has a stronger fragrance than flavor. To grow it indoors over winter, so you can use it fresh during the cold-weather months, take cuttings in July.

Lemon balm

Melissa officinalis

Perennial to Zone 5

Height: Up to 2^1/$_2$ feet

Lemon balm's heart-shaped leaves and minty lemon fragrance make it a popular herb in the garden as well as in teas and potpourri. And butterflies love lemon balm as much as people do. In some areas, it's invasive, so take precautions. (See page 17.)

Getting Started: In spring, sow seeds indoors or set out purchased plants in the garden. Space plants about 2 feet apart in full sun or partial shade and ordinary, well-drained soil with a neutral pH (7.0). Lemon balm will grow well in containers.

Growing: Cut back after flowering to avoid self-sowing. Mulch over winter. Propagate by taking cuttings in late spring or early summer, or dividing plants in spring. Remove unwanted self-sown plants.

Harvesting & Uses: Pinch off leaves as needed. Their fragrance is best when used fresh, but they may be dried or frozen. Use leaves in teas, cooking, potpourri, and sachets. Use for fragrance and to attract butterflies and bees.

Recommended Varieties: 'Variegata' and 'Aurea' have gold coloring in their leaves (they must be grown from cuttings or purchased plants). They may not be hardy in Zone 5.

Because of its fragrance, lemongrass is used commercially in soaps and perfumes. It's also grown to repel snakes and, in some parts of the world, lemongrass tea is drunk as an anti-depressant.

Lemongrass

Cymbopogon citrates

Annual except in Zones 9–11

Height: Up to 5 feet

For fans of Thai and other Southeast Asian cooking, lemongrass is an essential herb. As the name implies, it's an attractive, ornamental grass as well as an herb.

Getting Started: In late spring or early summer, plant in full sun and rich, well-drained, slightly acid soil. Or plant in a big container and take indoors in cold weather. (It will become dormant and regrow in spring.)

Growing: Fertilize monthly during the growing season. It's drought resistant and heat tolerant, but don't let soil of container plants dry out. When grown as a perennial, in spring of the second and following years, cut the plant back to 4 inches high before new growth begins. In Zones 7 and 8, you can cut the plant back to 12 inches high in fall and mulch heavily—often it returns in spring.

Harvesting & Uses: Cut fresh leaves and lower stems as needed. Wear gloves because of the leaves' sharp edges. You can refrigerate stems in a plastic bag for up to 2 weeks. Freeze stems or leaves for longer storage. Dry leaves on a screen for potpourri. Use in teas, Asian cooking, and potpourri.

Recommended Varieties: Indian lemongrass, *C. flexuosus*, is easy to grow.

Lemon verbena was introduced to the Old World by Spanish explorers, who found it growing in South America.

Lemon verbena

Aloysia triphylla

Annual except in Zones 9–11

Height: Up to 10 feet outdoors; 3 to 5 feet indoors

If you want intense lemon flavor, this South American native is for you. It's a deciduous shrub that can be grown in a container in cold climates and brought indoors during winter.

Getting Started: Plant in rich, moist but well-drained soil. The plant prefers full sun in cool or mild climates, but tolerates a little shade in hot climates. It can be started from seed, if available, but grows very slowly.

Growing: Fertilize once a month during the growing season. Make sure the soil of container-grown plants doesn't dry out. Water when rainfall is less than an inch per week. Remove faded flowers. Spray whiteflies, spider mites, or aphids with insecticidal soap. Cut back plants a few inches in spring to shape. Propagate by cuttings in late spring.

Harvesting & Uses: Use leaves fresh or dry them. Leaves are stiff and must be minced before using in cooking or removed from food before serving. Store dried leaves in an airtight container. Use in teas, potpourri, sachets, beverages, and salad dressings.

Recommended Varieties: No cultivars are readily available.

Licorice candy in the United States is generally not flavored with the herb licorice but with milder-tasting anise oil. In ancient China and Greece, licorice was often used to treat sore throats.

Licorice

Glycyrrhiza glabra

Perennial to Zone 5

Height: 3 to 4 feet

Licorice use has been recorded as far back as 3,000 years. The familiar flavoring comes from the plant's roots. (Fittingly, the botanical name of licorice means "sweet root.") The pea-like blooms add to its appeal.

Getting Started: Licorice may be grown from seeds started indoors in spring. Outdoors, place plants 3 feet apart in full sun to partial shade. Or plant pieces of root 6 inches deep and 3 feet from each other. Licorice prefers the sort of soil found in a good vegetable garden—rich, deep, and moisture retentive.

Growing: Licorice can be invasive; see page 17 for ways to control it. Water the plants when the soil dries. Fertilize monthly, especially plants growing in containers. In climates where temperatures go below freezing, mulch young plants over winter.

Harvesting & Uses: When the plant is 3 or 4 years old, dig up the roots in early winter. (Any left in the ground will sprout and create new plants.) Dry the roots for use in teas; they also have medicinal uses.

Recommended Varieties: No cultivars are readily available.

Mint

Mentha spp. and hybrids

Perennial to Zone 5

Height: 1 inch to 3 feet

Mint offers the best and the worst of the herb world. This is a very easy-to-grow group of plants that are highly fragrant and have lots of uses, from teas to baking and from potpourri to cosmetics. Like scented geraniums, mints come in many different flavors—apple, pineapple, ginger, grapefruit, and, always a favorite, chocolate. The downside is that mint is very aggressive and can easily take over a small garden. Even in a larger space, mint invades all corners, making plenty of work for the gardener who must dig it out over and over. But many growers can't resist at least one mint, so before you decide that you can't live without chocolate (or another) mint, turn to page 17 and read about strategies to handle invasive plants.

Getting Started: Place plants 2 to 3 feet apart in partial shade (although they'll tolerate full sun with no problems). Moist, well-drained soil is ideal. Container growing is highly recommended to help control them from spreading.

Growing: Don't let container plants dry out. In the garden, keep soil moist. For best flavor, fertilize lightly in late spring and early summer. Remove flowers (which are edible) to keep the plants from cross-pollinating, because the new plants created won't taste the same as those you planted. If a plant develops rust, remove it from the garden.

The only way to be sure you grow the particular type of mint that you want is to start with plants, not seeds. A remedy for chapped hands is to wash them in peppermint tea.

Harvesting & Uses: For fresh use, the best taste is obtained from sprigs at the top of the plant; pick them just before flowering. But leaves may be harvested at any time and frozen or dried for future use. Use leaves as flavorings for teas and other beverages and in vinegars, potpourri, and cosmetics. Flowers are useful in baked goods and may be crystallized.

Recommended Varieties: Since there are more than six hundred species and cultivars of mint and more being bred all the time, you'll find a wide choice. Here are a few you'll want to try: *Mentha* x *piperita* 'Chocolate'; *M. suaveolens* (apple mint, which doesn't need as much watering as most mints); *Mentha* x *piperita* (peppermint); *M. suaveolens* 'Variegata' (pineapple mint, which has cream and green leaves and may spread a bit less than most other mints); *Mentha spicata* (spearmint); *Mentha* x *gracilis* (ginger mint or Scottish mint, which has a more delicate flavor and variegated leaves); and *Mentha requienli* (Corsican mint, a tiny ground cover that prefers shade).

Add marjoram near the end of cooking to preserve its delicate flavor.

Marjoram

Origanum spp. and hybrids

Most are annuals; a few are perennials

Height: 10 to 14 inches

Marjoram is more than a milder version of oregano. It's an essential ingredient in Italian food and is one of the herbs that make up the French seasoning mix *fines herbes*.

Getting Started: In spring, after chance of frost has passed, sow seeds directly in the garden or set out plants 8 inches apart in full sun or partial shade. Because marjoram is native to rocky Mediterranean hillsides, it needs well-drained, slightly alkaline soil.

Growing: Marjoram is easy to grow in containers and indoors on a sunny windowsill. Fertilize container plants monthly. Water in the garden during dry spells.

Harvesting & Uses: Remove leaves for fresh use before the plant blooms. Later in the season, cut the top third of the stems and dry them by hanging or on a screen, removing leaves from the stems after they're dried. Use in cooking, aromatherapy, and potpourri; use plants to attract butterflies.

Recommended Varieties: *Origanum* x *majoricum* (hardy marjoram or Italian oregano) does better than sweet marjoram (*O. majorana*) in hot, humid climates. 'Kent Beauty' is colorful and perennial to Zone 6.

Mullein could be planted in a historic medicinal garden since it was used long ago to treat colds and congestion.

Mullein

Verbascum thapsus

Biennial (hardy to Zone 5)

Height: 5 to 6 feet

The leaves of mullein, which grows wild in many parts of the United States, may remind you of lamb's ears. But its flowers are much more attractive, and it doesn't mind hot and humid climates, as so many other silver-leaved plants do. However, it is invasive in some parts of the country.

Getting Started: Sow seeds indoors or directly in the ground in spring. Or start with transplants. Space about 24 inches apart in the garden. Although mullein prefers dry soil, it's adaptable. However, it needs to be placed in full sun. It's an eye-catching container plant.

Growing: Water plants during dry spells. Pick off caterpillars. Remove flowers before they go to seed to avoid the seeds scattering and becoming invasive. In some parts of North America, deer won't bother it.

Harvesting & Uses: Pick flowers as soon as they've opened. Use flowers in arrangements and cosmetics. A traditional use of the leaves was as a poultice for wounds. Plants are good for attracting butterflies and in the evening garden.

Recommended Varieties: Try *V. dumulsum* (dwarf mullein), which is a perennial.

Oregano

Origanum spp. and hybrids

Perennial to Zone 5

Height: 1 to 2 feet

It's easy to be confused by all the different plants called oregano. Many aren't true oreganos at all, but have the characteristic flavor that we recognize from spaghetti sauce. And you may have tried growing oregano (*Origanum vulgare*) and discovered that it was a disappointment; the dried leaves had little flavor. Sometimes, finding an oregano that has just the taste you like takes a bit of experimentation. You're more likely to be successful if you buy plants from a company that specializes in herbs. If you're buying locally (vs. buying from mail-order) crush a leaf from the plant before you buy. Some good cultivars for cooking (and other uses) are listed below.

Getting Started: In cold climates, set out plants in spring, after danger of frost has passed. Place plants 18 inches apart in well-drained soil that's in full sun or partial shade. (The best flavor is obtained from plants grown in full sun.) Oregano grows well in containers; place one near the kitchen door. In warmer climates, oregano can be planted throughout the growing season.

Growing: Water frequently until the plants are established. Fertilize once in early summer. If spider mites are a problem, spray with insecticidal soap. Cutting off the flowers will cause the plant to produce more leaves. Prune the plant to shape it after the flowers fade.

Harvesting & Uses: The tips of the stems have the best flavor, but for fresh use, cut any leaves when needed. They may be frozen or dried. Harvest flowers just as they open and dry them. Use in cooking, salads, vinegars, and butters; use the flowers fresh or dried.

Recommended Varieties: *O. vulgare* 'Italian' is excellent for cooking. If you want a stronger taste, try Greek oregano (*O. vulgare* subsp. *hirtum* 'Greek'). *O. vulgare* 'Aureum' and other gold oreganos aren't good in the kitchen, but are delightful ground covers (hardy to Zone 6) if given afternoon shade in hot climates. Dittany of Crete (*O. dictamnus*) is a short, creeping herb that must have very well-drained soil and afternoon shade. It has fuzzy gray foliage and interesting flowers, and is a good candidate for hanging baskets. It's hardy to Zone 6. What's called Mexican oregano (*Lippia graveolens*) isn't a true oregano but is a favorite with many cooks who favor spicy food.

Once upon a time, bald men mixed oregano with olive oil and slathered it on their heads in hopes of encouraging new hair to grow.

Nasturtium's leaves and flowers both taste peppery. Serve whole flowers in salads or as garnishes to meats and main dishes.

Nasturtium

Tropaeolum majus

Annual

Height: 18 inches

Nasturtium brightens up the herb garden, but that's not all. Both the colorful flowers and the peppery leaves are edible and a great choice for fresh salads, herbal vinegars, and as a spicy lettuce substitute on sandwiches.

Getting Started: In spring, sow seeds in poor to ordinary, well-drained soil after the last frost date. (In hot climates, grow as a fall and winter annual.) Place in full sun, except in hot climates, where partial shade is welcome. Nasturtiums have red, cream, yellow, or orange flowers and are vining or compact. Space vining cultivars 18 inches apart and compact plants 8 inches apart. Plants will grow in containers.

Growing: Do not fertilize, which increases leaf production and decreases flowers. Spray aphids with water, or use insecticidal soap. Remove faded flowers to keep plants blooming. Keep containers watered.

Harvesting & Uses: Pick flowers and leaves to use fresh. Use flowers and leaves for culinary purposes; use plants in landscaping and to attract hummingbirds.

Recommended Varieties: The Alaska series has variegated leaves.

Parsley is high in vitamins A, B, and C, and is an excellent source of iron.

Parsley

Petroselinum crispum

Biennial

Height: 12 to 20 inches

Parsley is a well-known garnish, but it also enhances the taste and nutritional value of many foods. it appears in the French seasonings *fines herbes* and bouquet garni.

Getting Started: To speed seed germination, soak seeds overnight in warm water before sowing indoors, or nick each seed with a file. Or start with purchased plants of either flat-leaf (Italian) or curled (French) parsley. (Flat-leaf is easier to grow in hot, humid climates.) Provide rich, moist soil. Parsley can tolerate more shade than many other herbs.

Growing: Keep the soil moist, especially during the plant's second summer, as it will slow flowering and bolting (going to seed). Fertilize several times during the growing season. Remove slugs. Parsley grows nicely in containers and may be grown indoors on a bright windowsill if kept well watered. Pick off caterpillars by hand and move them to another plant, leaving some on the parsley, as they are the larvae of the anise swallowtail butterfly.

Harvesting & Uses: Pick leaves as needed for fresh use or freezing. Use in cooking and as a breath freshener.

Recommended Varieties: Try 'Triplex' and 'Catalogno'.

Dry pot marigold flowers on paper towels placed on top of a screen. Dry each petal separately so they won't discolor one another when they touch..

Pot marigold

Calendula officinalis

Annual

Height: Up to 2 feet

Flower gardeners call this pretty flowering plant calendula, but herbalists know it best as pot marigold. It's not the type of marigold commonly seen in summer yards, although it does have yellow, gold, red, or orange flowers. The blooms have a peppery taste and can be substituted for expensive saffron in cooking.

Getting Started: In cool climates, sow seeds indoors or outdoors several weeks before the last frost date. Or buy as a bedding plant. Pot marigold prefers full sun and well-drained soil, but tolerates some shade in warmer climates. Space 9 to 12 inches apart. In areas with hot summers, plant in fall instead of spring. It is a good container plant.

Growing: Fertilize once in late spring. Water during dry spells. Remove faded flowers to prolong blooming. Remove slugs and spray aphids with water from the hose.

Harvesting & Uses: Pick flowers as they open; use fresh or dry. Cut leaves for culinary use when they're young and tender. Use in potpourri, cooking, and vinegars.

Recommended Varieties: 'Pacific Beauty' and 'Indian Prince' have large flowers. The Bon Bon series is short and blooms early.

Once upon a time, rosemary flowers were white, not blue. But when Mary, Joseph, and baby Jesus were fleeing into Egypt, Mary hid behind a rosemary shrub to evade some soldiers. When she emerged, the flowers turned from white to blue, to honor her.

Rosemary

Rosmarinus officinalis

Perennial to Zone 8; annual in colder climates

Height: Up to 4 feet

Not so long ago, rosemary wasn't very hardy, but now cold-tolerant cultivars are available. When I lived in Boston, rosemary was the one herb I could count on returning every year. And when I moved to South Carolina, I found a small hedge of it in my backyard. Yea!

Getting Started: There are trailing and upright forms. Look also for cultivars with pink, blue, or white flowers, all of which are edible. Buy plants in spring because the seeds can be hard to germinate. Place them 12 to 24 inches apart in full sun in ordinary, well-drained soil with a neutral pH (7.0). It's a good container plant.

Growing: Water young plants during dry spells. Pot up and bring indoors over winter in cold climates. Propagate by taking cuttings in spring or layering in summer.

Harvesting & Uses: Cut leaves as needed and blooms as they open. May be dried or frozen. Use in cooking, grilling, vinegars, and potpourri; use dried and crystallized flowers.

Recommended Varieties: 'Arp' and 'Hill Hardy' withstand cold well. 'Prostratus' and 'Blue Boy' are compact.

Sage and Salvias

Salvia spp. and hybrids

Most are perennial to Zone 5

Height: Up to 3 feet

If sage comes to mind only at Thanksgiving and in connection with turkey dressing, boy, are you in for a surprise! The common garden sage used for cooking (*Salvia officinalis*) has turned into an ornamental plant with leaves that are purple or brightly variegated. But beyond that, how about the salvias that attract hummingbirds with their brilliant red flowers? There are so many varieties of sage that it's hard to keep track of them. You'll definitely want to try pineapple sage, *Salvia elegans*, even though it's an annual in climates colder than Zone 8. Grow it in a pot on your deck or patio and place an electric fan behind it when people are around—everyone will want to know where the pineapple fragrance is coming from.

Getting Started: Place plants 18 to 24 inches apart in full sun and ordinary, well-drained soil. Sage is an excellent container plant.

Growing: Trim plants occasionally to keep them compact and prevent them from flopping over. Always trim in spring to encourage new growth. Water container plants regularly. Ornamental sages require more water than culinary ones. Watch out for red spider mites on container-grown plants and treat with insecticidal soap. Mulch over winter.

In ancient times, sage was considered to confer long life on those who consumed it, and its name comes from the Latin word for "salvation."

Harvesting & Uses: Pick leaves as needed. Harvest flowers just as they open. Both may be dried, but the taste of fresh is best. Use in cooking, baking, vinegars, and cosmetics.

Recommended Varieties: *Salvia elegans* (pineapple sage) has red flowers and a wonderful aroma. Use it in teas and potpourri. Try these colorful cultivars of garden sage: *S. officinalis* 'Tricolor', which has pink, cream, and green leaves; *S. officinalis* 'Purpurea', which has purple leaves; and *S. officinalis* 'Icterina', which has gold and green foliage. Although they add interest to the garden, all are good for cooking too. Clary sage (*S. sclarea*) produces impressive 4-foot spikes of blue, purple, or white flowers. *S. coccinea* is an ornamental sage or saliva that's a hummingbird magnet. Silver sage (*S. argentea*) is a biennial with silver leaves. Spanish sage (*S. lavandulifolia*) has a very strong flavor and is evergreen to Zone 5. Fruit-scented sage (*S. dorisiana*) has large lime green leaves and a very strong and delightful fragrance.

Leonardo da Vinci said that eating rue gave him clearer eyesight. But being out in the sun a long time after consuming rue can cause strong sunburn.

Rue

Ruta graveolens

Perennial to Zone 4

Height: Up to 3 feet

Evergreen rue—also known as the herb of grace—is an attractive addition to the herb garden because of its bluish foliage and its historical significance. (It's mentioned both in the Bible and by Shakespeare.) The yellow flowers are a nice contrast to the leaves.

Getting Started: Buy plants in spring and place them 18 inches apart in ordinary, well-drained soil with a neutral pH (7.0). Rue prefers full sun but will grow in partial shade. It grows well in containers. Because of its bluish foliage, it looks nice near gray plants.

Growing: Water during dry spells. Cut back the plant in the second and following springs to encourage new growth. Propagate by division in spring or layering in summer.

Harvesting & Uses: Wear gloves when harvesting as some people have skin that's irritated by the leaves. Pick leaves before the plant blooms and remove seedpods when they're brown and ripe. Use seedpods in crafts; dried leaves may repel insects.

Recommended Varieties: 'Jackman's Blue' has intense blue foliage. 'Variegata' offers interesting white variegation on the leaves. 'Blue Curl' has curly foliage.

If using salad burnet as an edging, cut off the tall flower stalks that appear in spring.

Salad burnet

Sanguisorba minor

Perennial to Zone 4

Height: Up to 2 feet

This uncommon evergreen herb tastes a bit like cucumber. Some people note a slightly nutty flavor. But this favorite of the Pilgrims isn't the best choice for growing in the hottest climates.

Getting Started: Sow seeds indoors in spring, 6 to 8 weeks before the last frost. Transplant outdoors and place 8 to 12 inches apart in average, well-drained soil. Salad burnet grows well in containers, but care should be taken not to overwater. It also makes a nice edging plant for the borders of the herb garden.

Growing: Because salad burnet is drought tolerant, it rarely needs watering. Don't fertilize, as that makes the leaves too soft. Remove flowers to prevent the plant from self-sowing and to keep the herb's flavor strong. Salad burnet may be divided in early autumn to increase your supply of plants.

Harvesting & Uses: Pick tender young leaves year-round for fresh use. Cut flowers as they open. Use in cooking, salads, and vinegars.

Recommended Varieties: No cultivars are readily available.

Historically, summer and winter savory were considered to affect libido. Summer savory was said to increase ardor and winter savory to lessen it.

Savory, summer

Satureja hortensis

Annual

Height: Up to 18 inches

Herb gardeners can choose from two types of savory. Summer savory is an annual; winter savory is a perennial. Summer savory is slightly taller and has a more delicate flavor. And the leaves of summer savory are a lighter color. Both have white or lavender flowers.

Getting Started: Set plants in the garden after chance of frost has passed in spring. Space them 10 to 12 inches apart in full sun and good, well-drained soil. To keep the harvest going through fall, start a second crop in early summer. Summer savory is a good container plant.

Growing: Don't fertilize or the plant will flop over. It tolerates dry conditions, but water it during droughts. Poor drainage will lead to root rot. Pinch back stems to keep the plant compact.

Harvesting & Uses: The leaves are most flavorful before the plant flowers. Use fresh or dry. Use leaves in teas and cooking; cook them with beans to reduce flatulence. Summer savory is one of the herbs in the classic *herbes de Provence*. Use plants to attract butterflies.

Recommended Varieties: No cultivars are readily available.

Winter savory is considered drought tolerant. It will rot, however, if drainage—especially in winter—is poor.

Savory, winter

Satureja montana

Perennial to Zone 5

Height: 12 inches

Winter savory is evergreen in mild climates and semievergreen elsewhere, which adds to its appeal. It is an excellent landscape plant and was once used in love potions.

Getting Started: Set out plants in spring after frost has passed. Choose a sunny spot with very well-drained soil. Avoid clay soil, which can lead to rotting, especially over winter and particularly for creeping forms. Space about 8 inches apart. Grow winter savory in a raised bed or a container if drainage is poor.

Growing: Water when rainfall is less than an inch per week. Trim regularly to keep the plant shaped and to encourage new growth. Mulch over winter. Propagate by cuttings.

Harvesting & Uses: Cut leaves for fresh use as needed. Leaves may be refrigerated in a plastic bag. Their flavor will be better if harvesting takes place before the plant flowers. Leaves become very hard when they're dried. Use leaves in cooking, teas, and salads. Use plants to attract butterflies and in knot gardens.

Recommended Varieties: *S. montana* 'Procumbens' is a nice creeping form. *S. montana* 'Nana' is an attractive dwarf.

In the Middle Ages, sweet woodruff was often used as a filler for mattresses and to strew on floors as a natural air freshener. If you need a plant that will grow in dry shade beneath trees, sweet woodruff fills the bill.

Sweet woodruff

Galium odoratum

Perennial to Zone 4

Height: 12 inches

If your garden receives too little sun, here's the herb for you. Sweet woodruff doesn't just tolerate partial shade—it prefers full shade. In a woodland garden, it is an attractive ground cover with small white flowers in spring, but it may be invasive.

Getting Started: Place sweet woodruff plants about 8 inches apart in a shady spot that has rich, moisture-retaining but well-drained soil. They perform best in alkaline soil, but are adaptable. They will grow happily beneath trees if they receive some spring moisture. For container growing, use a large pot so the plant doesn't quickly become root-bound.

Growing: In hot climates, mulch plants slightly and water occasionally to keep them from going dormant in summer. Watch out for runners that creep into other areas of the garden and pull them up.

Harvesting & Uses: Cut leaves and flowers as needed and dry them. They have an aroma like vanilla or new-mown hay. Use in potpourri, sachets, and aromatherapy, and for fragrance.

Recommended Varieties: No cultivars are readily available.

Tansy's unusual feathery leaves are pine-scented. Although once used as a folk remedy, it's now known to be toxic if ingested.

Tansy

Tanacetum vulgare

Perennial to Zone 4

Height: 3 to 4 feet

Although tansy is not edible, its bright yellow flowers make it a colorful choice for the herb garden and for use in crafts.

Getting Started: In spring, sow seeds indoors and transplant into a spot with full sun and ordinary, very well-drained soil. Space 3 feet apart. Tansy is a good candidate for container growing because it spreads by runners and can become invasive. (See page 17.)

Growing: Knock off aphids with a strong blast of water from the hose. Cut the plant back a bit after it flowers to encourage a more compact habit. Dig up plants that have grown out of bounds. Pile them on the compost pile, where they'll add potassium. To increase your supply of plants, divide in spring or early fall. Mulch in winter.

Harvesting & Uses: Cut leaves as needed and flowers just after they've opened. Dry them for later use. Use in flower arrangements, potpourri, and insect repellent.

Recommended Varieties: *T. vulgare* 'Crispum' is shorter than average and has curlier leaves. *T. vulgare* 'Isala Gold' has golden foliage, and *T. vulgare* 'Silver Lace' is variegated.

Thyme

Thymus spp. and hybrids

Perennial (most are hardy to Zone 4; exceptions noted below)

Height: 1 to 18 inches

Thymes are a large and diverse group of plants. Appearance, flavor, size, fragrance, and growth habit vary widely. There are too many species and cultivars to mention, but you'll find recommendations below to get you started. You'll discover thymes that are grown for kitchen use and those that are strictly ornamental. A further distinction is between thymes that grow upright and creeping thymes, which make great ground covers and grow well between steppingstones in a pathway. All attract bees and make good honey.

Getting Started: Common thyme (*Thymus vulgaris*) may be started from seed indoors about 6 weeks before the last frost date. With all other thymes, buy plants. Place in sun or partial shade in ordinary, or even poor, well-drained soil. Space 6 to 16 inches apart. Thyme grows well in raised beds, containers, and rock gardens. In containers and raised beds, mix soil with one-third fine bark to increase drainage.

Growing: Let the soil surface dry before watering. Trim back after flowering to prevent the plant from becoming too woody and to encourage new growth. If aphids are troublesome on new growth, wash off with a strong blast of water from the hose or spray insecticidal soap. Mulch less-hardy plants in late fall. Plants will rot over winter if the soil is too wet.

Harvesting & Uses: Cut leaves and flowers as needed. The flavor is best just before the plant blooms. Dry by hanging or on a screen. Strip the dried leaves and flowers from the stem and store them in a plastic bag. Use flowers and leaves in cooking, teas, and wreaths. Use plants in landscaping.

Recommended Varieties: *T. vulgaris* 'Silver Posie' has attractive variegated leaves and excellent flavor. Other good culinary choices are 'English' thyme, which grows vigorously and has shiny foliage, and 'Narrow-leaf French', which has silvery leaves and a spicier taste. *Thymus pulegioides* 'Aureus' or golden thyme (Zone 5) combines gold leaves with pink flowers. Some attractive creeping thymes are *T. serpyllum* 'Annie Hall', *T. serpyllum* 'Lemon Curd', and 'Snowdirft'. Camphor thyme (*T. camphoratus*) is often used to repel moths. Most of the lemon thymes (*T.* x *citriodorus*) are winter hardy only to Zone 6, but are worth growing as annuals. *T.* x *citriodorus* 'Argenteus' is a lemon thyme with lovely silver foliage. *T.* x *citriodorus* 'Silver Queen' is evergreen to Zone 6. *T. herba-barona* is caraway flavored.

Make sure that thyme doesn't suffer from wet feet over winter; that causes them to rot. All thymes do better in soil that's low in nutrients than in rich soil, which causes soft growth, attracts aphids, and decreases flavor.

The story goes that England's King Henry VIII divorced Catherine of Aragon (wife number one) for using too much tarragon.

Tarragon

Artemisia dracunculus

Perennial to Zone 4

Height: 2 feet

French tarragon is an herb best suited to cool climates, Zones 3-5, or other areas with mild summers. In hot summer weather, it goes dormant. *Tagetes lucida*, Mexican mint marigold, has a tarragon flavor and is a good substitute for Zones 6-10.

Getting Started: Start with plants in early spring, as seeds of true French tarragon aren't available. Place them 2 feet apart in full sun and moisture-holding soil. Tarragon makes a good container plant.

Growing: Water weekly if rainfall is less than an inch. Fertilize if leaves yellow. Poorly draining soil will cause the plant to rot. Divide plants in spring to increase your supply. Mulch over winter.

Harvesting & Uses: Cut anytime after the stems are 6 or more inches long. The leaves taste best early in the season. Dry or freeze for later use. Use in cooking, grilling, salad dressings, vinegars, and marinades.

Recommended Varieties: Smell a leaf before you buy to make sure you're getting true French tarragon (which is propagated vegetatively) and not Russian tarragon, which is vastly inferior and has little flavor.

Yarrow is a good choice for gardens with sandy soil. In Victorian flower language, yarrow flowers signified "war," which is how gardeners may feel when a plant spreads by runners where it isn't wanted.

Yarrow

Achillea millefolium

Perennial to Zone 3

Height: 3 feet

We know that yarrow has been around for more than 60,000 years. And in all that time, it hasn't lost any of its popularity.

Getting Started: In late spring, sow seeds indoors or outside in the garden. Place the plants 12 inches apart in a spot with full sun and good drainage. Yarrow is a nice container plant. Choose among new cultivars with flowers that are pink, red, and peach as well as yellow and gold. Many new cultivars grow shorter than older types.

Growing: This plant is drought tolerant, although it performs better if watered during dry spells. Remove faded flowers to keep the plant blooming. Yarrow may be invasive. It has creeping rhizomes and self-sows. Be diligent in removing unwanted plants. Divide the plant in spring or early fall.

Harvesting & Uses: Pick flowers when they're fully opened. Dry by hanging. Use as cut flowers and in potpourri. Use plants in nighttime gardens and to attract butterflies.

Recommended Varieties: *A.* x 'Coronation Gold' never flops over and is excellent for drying. *A. tomentosa*, woolly yarrow, is good as a ground cover and in a rock garden.

Herb Gardens

If you've become so enthusiastic about herb theme gardens that a baker's dozen isn't enough, here are twenty-three additional ideas for culinary, historic, and fun herb gardens.

Herb Garden for Italian Cooking

Grow the herbs that are most used in Italian food: basil, bay, garlic, Greek oregano, parsley, rosemary, sage, and thyme.

Herb Garden for Thai Cooking

The herbs used in Thai cooking require a warm summer: basil (including holy basil), cumin, ginger, hot peppers, and lemongrass. (Ginger grows best in areas with mild climates, but may be grown in a container and overwintered in a greenhouse. You can plant a root from the grocery store in early summer.)

Herb Garden for French Cooking

The herbs you'll need for classic French cooking include basil, chervil, marjoram, mint, rosemary, sage, and thyme. You can add bay, if you have room for it and like it.

Herbes de Provence Garden

This is a variation on the French cooking garden that's good for warm climates. Grow the herbs that make up the classic recipe for the seasoning mixture *herbes de Provence*: basil, fennel, rosemary, summer savory, and thyme.

Colonial American Herb Garden

These are the plants that were growing in New England herb gardens by the 1670s: cilantro/coriander, feverfew, parsley, pot marigold, santolina, sorrel, and winter savory. (Sorrel is a tart, lemon-flavored perennial herb that likes moist soil. Santolina, known as lavender cotton, is an evergreen shrub with gray leaves. It needs full sun and well-drained soil.)

Shaker Herb Garden

Although the Shakers grew various herbs at different times and locations, a basic Shaker herb garden would contain basil, borage, horehound, hyssop, sage, tansy, and thyme.

Salsa Garden

This is an easy and fun garden for those who like to cook. Start with the plants in the pizza garden (page 40) and add cucumbers, cantaloupe, and watermelon. (If you're short on space, grow the cukes up a tomato cage made of concrete reinforcing wire and grow dwarf varieties of the melons.)

People tend either to love or hate the taste of cilantro/coriander. Those who aren't fond of it will be pleased to know that the name coriander comes from a Greek word that means "bug" because of the aroma of its leaves.

Zoo Herb Garden for Kids

This garden contains herbs and other plants that have the names of animals: bee balm (bergamot), catnip, dandelion, hens and chickens, horehound, and lamb's ears. (As any homeowner knows, dandelions are easy to start from the seeds in the plant's puffballs. Hens and chickens is the common name of *Sempervivum tectorum*, a succulent perennial plant that likes well-drained soil.)

Sunflower Herb House for Kids

Make a tepee of wooden stakes and tie them at the top. Plant a sunflower seed at the base of each. After they start to grow, train them to grow up the stakes. Around the base of the tepee, plant alpine strawberries (kids love to eat them) and bergamot or pineapple sage to attract hummingbirds.

"When in Rome" Herb Garden

The Romans grew many herbs, so you have a wide choice. Pick a traditional geometric design for this garden—a circle of lavender around a dozen individual plants, or an oblong bed surrounded by brick paving and ornamented by a small fountain or birdbath. Plant the herbs in a symmetrical pattern. Some choices: bay, caraway, Roman chamomile, cilantro/coriander, dill, hyssop, lavender, licorice, parsley, rue, and winter savory.

Herb Rock Garden

Herbs that prefer well-drained soil and like sun are good candidates for a traditional rock garden. Some suggestions: artemisia, chives, garlic chives, lavender, rosemary, sage, santolina, summer savory, creeping thyme, and yarrow.

Herb Garden to Dye For

Down through the ages, herbs have been used to produce the rich colors of natural dyes. You can experiment with these: *Anthemis tinctoria* (known as dyer's chamomile, its flowers produce a bright yellow color when mixed with alum); pot marigold (green dye comes from the leaves, pale yellow from the flowers); parsley (green); sorrel (pale yellow); and tansy (yellow).

Victorian Herb Garden

Do you have a Victorian-style home? Plant an herb garden that includes plants popular during Victorian days: bergamot, feverfew, horehound, lamb's ears, nasturtium, pot marigold, rosemary, sweet woodruff, and verbena. Fancy garden ornaments, gazebos, iron fences, and symmetrical beds were popular elements of Victorian garden design.

Salad Herb Garden

Many herbs make tasty additions to salads. Some that you may want to try: anise, basil, borage, chervil, chives, dill, fennel, garlic chives, lemon balm, marjoram, nasturtium, oregano, parsley, salad burnet, savory, tarragon, and thyme.

Indian Herb Garden

Fans of Indian food might want to grow some of the herbs that contribute to the distinctive taste of the various regional cuisines of India: basil, cilantro/coriander, cumin, garlic, mint, mustard, and parsley. And be sure to plant a few fiery chile pepper plants among them!

Asian Herb Garden

The cuisines of Asia vary quite a bit according to country, but they have some common elements: bay, basils (sweet basil, Thai basil, and holy basil), cilantro, garlic chives, lemongrass (you can substitute lemon balm or lemon verbena), and mint. And don't forget chile plants, for their pods and leaves.

July Fourth Herb Garden

Red, white, and blue are always popular but never more so than around the midsummer celebration of American independence. Bergamot, roses, and nasturtiums produce red flowers. White can come from basil, garlic chives, scented geraniums, roses, and some yarrows. Blue is tricky because there's a fine line between blue and lavender, so try to see the plant in bloom first, if possible. Look among cultivars of these plants to find the color blue: anise hyssop, borage, catnip, hyssop, lavender, rosemary, and sage.

Lavender Lovers Herb Garden

There are at least 28 species and numerous cultivars of lavender. How many do you have room for? Maybe you'd like to try lavenders with flowers that aren't purple. For white flowers, consider *Lavendula angustifolia* 'Alba' and 'Dutch White'; for pink blooms, *Lavendula angustifolia* 'Rosea' and 'Hidcote Pink'. Or you could try to grow English lavender (*Lavendula angustifolia*) and French lavender (*Lavendula stoechas*, which also offers some plants with white and pink flowers, as well as the usual purple and bluish). Another species, *Lavendula dentata*, sometimes is called French lavender and sometimes, Spanish lavender. It isn't bothered by humidity, as many lavenders are, but it's killed by frost.

Alphabet Herbs

This can be fun for a kid's garden. Grow a garden of herbs whose names start with the same letters as your child's (or your) first or last name. SAM = savory, anise, and yarrow. SMITH = Sweet woodruff, monarda, indigo, tansy, and horehound. Sometimes, if you can't find common names that start with a letter in a name, look at the botanical names to see if you can find a match. For example, if you need a "p," the botanical name of anise is *Pimpinella anisum*. In SMITH, we used monarda instead of bergamot.

Rainbow Herb Garden

You can find all the colors of the rainbow—red, orange, yellow, green, blue, indigo, and violet—in either herb flowers or foliage. Here's one possibility: pineapple sage (red), nasturtium (orange), yarrow (yellow), parsley (green), borage (blue), indigo (lavender), and violets. Consider planting a rainbow herb garden in the traditional rainbow arc shape.

Edible Flowers Herb Garden

Since most herbs are grown to be eaten, why not have a small herb garden that contains only edible herb flowers? Please *do* eat the flowers of bergamot, chives, dill, fennel, garlic chives, lavender, mint, pineapple sage, pot marigold, roses, and violets.

One-Color Herb Garden

Pick your favorite color and grow a garden of herbs that have flowers in that single hue. Note that various cultivars of some herbs will vary from the colors they're listed with:

Blue: Anise hyssop, borage, hyssop, sage, rosemary

Orange: Nasturtium, pot marigold

Pink: Basil (several types), bergamot, hyssop

Purple/Lavender: Chives, lavender, mints, violets

Red: Bergamot, nasturtium, pineapple sage (and some other ornamental salvias), roses

White: Basil, caraway, chamomile, garlic chives, roses, some scented geraniums

Yellow: Dill, lady's mantle, pot marigold, rue, tansy, yarrow

A Harry Potter Herb Garden

Historically, many herbs were believed to have magical properties—to ward off witches, for instance, or as potions. Here are a few that might have been grown in an herb garden at Hogwarts:

Caraway—used to protect from the evil eye; also in love potions

Chamomile—for luck

Dill—protect against witchcraft and encourage romance

Fennel—repel witches

Garlic—ward off evil spirits and as a potion to increase courage

Horseradish—to ensure prosperity

Oregano—protect from evil spirits

Marjoram—to attract a husband

Pot marigold—to make dreams come true

Rosemary—protection for babies; extend youthful appearance for women

Spearmint—to make wishes come true

Thyme—protect against witches

Preserving
Herbs

Once you grow your own herbs, you'll never lack enough oregano to make as much marinara sauce as you want, even if it's January. And you won't need to buy artemisia for an impromptu wreath you decide to assemble for Valentine's Day. Preserving herbs gives you an ample supply year-round. And it isn't hard at all. You can dry or freeze herbs several different ways.

Drying

Air drying is the simplest way to preserve herbs. Just spread them out on screens or hang them in a warm, dark place with good air circulation. Try these techniques:

- Hanging works best with herbs that have long stems. Gather small bundles of stems and fasten them together at the bottom with rubber bands (which will contract as the plants dry). If you're drying plants with seeds, cover the flowers with a paper bag in which you've punched small holes and fasten with a rubber band. As the seeds dry, they will fall into the bag and not on the floor.
- Many herbs also dry well when spread out on screens. Just be sure you don't put the screens in the sun—that adversely affects color.
- If you have a few herbs you need to dry during a rainy time, use a gas oven with a pilot light. Spread the herbs lightly and evenly over cookie sheets and place in the oven. (Don't turn it on.) Stir daily. They should be dry in several days.

- Food dehydrators are also handy for drying many herbs. The color of the dried herbs will be excellent and usually the flavor will be too. But some herbs, such as basil, lose flavor in a dehydrator. Follow the manufacturer's directions.
- One of the most unusual drying techniques is also the easiest—spread herbs on a cake cooling rack and place in a frost-free refrigerator. That's it. Do not cover the herbs. It takes about a week—occasionally longer—for them to dry, but check daily to be sure.
- Store whole dried herbs in dark glass jars with lids, and use within a year.

Freezing

Freezing is better than drying for preserving the flavor of some herbs. Basil, chives, dill, chervil, fennel, mint, parsley, and tarragon all retain flavor better when frozen. Here's how:
- Cut clean, dry herbs into small pieces and put them into plastic freezer bags. Seal inside a second freezer bag, label, and use within 6 months. (You can also use small plastic freezer containers with lids, but exclude as much air as possible.)
- Blend a quantity of fresh herbs in a blender or food processor. Place in the individual compartments of an ice cube tray and fill to the top with water. Freeze. When frozen, remove from the trays and place in freezer bags. Be sure to label them so you'll

know which green cubes are mint and which are basil! These can be dropped, still frozen, into stews, soups, and other dishes as they cook.

- Some herbalists like to freeze herbs in an oil paste. Blend 2 cups of fresh herbs in a blender or food processor, then slowly add ½ cup vegetable oil until it's mixed. If you're not going to use this the day you prepare it, it must be frozen. Otherwise there's a chance botulism-causing bacteria could grow in it. Freeze the herb-oil paste in small quantities, such as in ice cube trays, and then repackage in plastic bags or freezer containers.

One More Idea

Although this suggestion doesn't preserve herbs for long periods, it does keep them fresh for a week or so. It's especially recommended for basil and parsley, which don't take well to refrigeration. Simply place the stems of the herbs in a glass or vase filled with a few inches of water and place on the kitchen counter. Take care to remove any leaves that would be underwater. Then change the water daily and enjoy your fresh herbs.

Flowers

These herb flowers can be used in salads, served as garnishes, and sprinkled over various dishes. Be sure that none have been touched by pesticides and that you wash the blossoms well.

Anise hyssop
Basil, holy
Bergamot
Borage
Caraway
Catnip
Chamomile
Chervil
Chives
Dill
Fennel
Geranium, scented
Hyssop
Lavender
Lemon verbena
Marjoram
Mint
Mustard
Nasturtium
Oregano
Pot marigold
Rose
Salad burnet
Summer savory
Sweet woodruff
Tarragon

Fun Things
to Do With Herbs

How to Make Money With Herbs

Once you're growing a good-sized herb garden, you may find that you have more dried herbs and more plants than you know what to do with. If so, maybe you'd like to try to earn some extra cash through your herbs. Here are some ideas:

- Sell top-quality fresh herbs to local chefs. Talk to some and find out what they use most.
- Pot up and sell extra plants. Try offering moss-lined hanging baskets of herbs or larger containers of several herbs, for example, a container garden of herbs for French or Italian cooking. You could also market small plants for party favors or for take-home centerpieces.
- Design and plant herb gardens for others. You could also offer a weekly maintenance service for the gardens.
- Create your own seasoning blends of dried herbs, package the blends attractively, and find a gift shop that will carry your products.
- Create various blends of potpourri, package them in attractive containers of various sizes, and sell them for gifts or home use. Make one a citrusy holiday blend for December sales.
- Make an herb tossing mixture for weddings, to replace the usual rice or confetti.
- Save seeds of those herbs that readily produce lots of seeds and package them in colorful packets.
- Sell homemade wreaths covered with dried herbs. Offer several sizes and colors, or seasonal themes.
- Create and sell closet angels, herbal tea mixtures, sachets, and bath sachets. Or make and sell herbal vinegars. Often these products can be targeted at birthday parties, baby showers, anniversaries, bridal showers, and other occasions, as well as at the gift market.

Herbal Gift Ideas

Anyone with an herb garden has plenty of material at hand to create unique gifts for friends and family.

- Make "closet angels" filled with sweet-smelling or moth-repelling potpourri. Use a Christmas angel cookie cutter about 3 inches tall to cut two pieces of pretty fabric into angel shapes. Sew the shapes together, leaving an opening for the potpourri. Fill the angel with the potpourri and hand-sew the fabric closed. Add a ribbon on top so the angel can hang from a closet rod.

- Mix up a favorite dried herbal tea mix and place on a piece of plastic wrap. Gather the edges of the plastic wrap into a packet and tie it at the top with a pretty ribbon. Attach a card explaining what the mixture is and give directions for how to brew a cup of tea. Package in a pretty teacup, maybe an antique one that you picked up at a flea market.

- Package several of your favorite blends of dried cooking herbs and label attractively. Place in a basket with several useful cooking utensils.

- Using fancy fabric, create a one-of-a-kind cover for a toss pillow. Insert the pillow in the case and add a removable sachet so you can change the scents or refresh the aroma.

- Make a special bath sachet by gathering pretty nonshrinking fabric around dried lavender, rosemary, and rose petals. Tie at the top with an attractive ribbon that's long enough to hang below the bath faucet so the hot water can run through the sachet as the tub fills. (These sachets can be dried after the first use and used once more.)

- Make a pint of herb-flavored honey by mixing 1 tablespoon fresh herbs or 1 teaspoon dried (or more to taste) into a 16-ounce jar of honey.

- As a present for a favorite home cook, make herbal salts to flavor food by mixing equal parts of fresh herbs and salt. (Sea salt is good for this.) If all you have are dried herbs, use 6 to 8 tablespoons dried herbs to 1 cup salt. Put the salt and herbs in a blender or food processor and blend until well mixed, about 2 minutes. Spread on a cookie sheet and bake in the oven at 200 degrees F for about 1 hour, stirring frequently. Let cool, stir, and put in glass jars. Label.
- Homemade herb butter (perhaps packaged in an old-fashioned butter mold) makes a great culinary gift. Blend 1 stick butter with 1 teaspoon lemon juice and 1 tablespoon fresh herbs or 2 teaspoons dried herbs. Yield: about ½ cup.

An Herb-Themed Wedding and a Wedding Herb Toss

Brides often look for a pretty garden in which to say "I do." Why not carry that garden theme throughout the engagement and wedding by using fragrant herbs and their flowers in numerous ways? This fits nicely with the concept of "green" weddings, which are all the rage now, since natural herbs are very environmentally friendly.

Wedding Herb Toss

Whether brides plan to have an herbal theme for the wedding or not, tossing a colorful and sweet-smelling mixture of herbs and roses—instead of rice or confetti—has become quite popular. It's more natural, it's better for the environment, and it leaves the wedding venue delightfully fragrant.

The herb mixture can be as elaborate or as simple as you like. And you can personalize it with your choice of herbs as well as the colors and pattern of the cones or holders. Here's an example of one recipe:

6 cups dried rose petals
6 cups dried lavender buds

¹/₂ cup dried grated orange or lemon peel

2 cups scented geranium leaves (optional)

This makes enough to fill about 35 to 50 decorative cones that can be given to guests. You can vary the proportions to make more or less, depending on the number of guests.

The Language of Flowers

Typically, the bride chooses the herbs and flowers according to her colors and fragrances, paying attention to their meanings in the Victorian language of flowers. Here are just a few:

Chamomile = Patience in adversity

Lavender = Devotion

Marjoram = Joy and happiness

Rose = Undying love

Rosemary = Remembrance

The Holders

You can make cones of cellophane, organza, heavy decorative paper, or other stiff material in a pattern that matches the wedding colors and fill them with the herb mixture. This makes it easy for guests to toss the herbs. Count on $1/4$ to $1/3$ cup of fresh herbs for each, depending on the size of the cones (usually 3 x 5 inches or 4 x 7 inches). An alternative is to fill big crystal bowls with the mix and place them near the exit the bridal couple will use. Put a few long-handled spoons in each bowl for ease of use. You may also want to have some sachets of the mix on trays nearby for guests to take home.

Ways to Extend the Herbal Wedding Theme

- Use small potted herbs as table favors at a shower, the bridesmaids' luncheon, or a sit-down wedding dinner.
- Make small sachets of the wedding toss for favors. Tie with a pretty ribbon or raffia.
- Include a fresh sprig of whichever herb is chosen to be the theme in the bride's and bridesmaids' bouquets, as well as the flower girl's tussie-mussie (nosegay) and the groom's and groomsmen's boutonnieres.
- Strew the cake table with rose petals and lavender.
- Have the bride wear a head wreath of herbs, as brides often did in the past.

- Providing it's okay with the church or other venue, have the flower girl lightly toss dried lavender as she comes down the aisle.
- Place stems of fresh or dried lavender in vases throughout the wedding or reception site. Alternatively, throughout the area, place bowls of the dried herb mix used for the wedding toss.
- Add a pinch of the herbs chosen for the wedding toss mix to the invitations and the thank-you notes.
- Use herb flowers or rose petals to decorate the cake,
- Hang herb wreaths as decorations at the reception.

How to Make Herb Wreaths

What a pleasure it is to have fragrant wreaths in the entryway to welcome guests, in the kitchen to pluck herbs for a delicious sauce, and anywhere in the home you want sweet scents and a natural accent. Start with a frame of grapevine, straw, wire, or heavy foam. Then gather a variety of fresh or dried herbs and dried flowers of differing textures. Choose a color scheme ahead of time—maybe pink and green or lavender and silver. Gather herbs and flowers into bundles 3 to 5 inches long. Tie them at the base with thin wire or florist tape. Begin covering the form on the inside rim, working in one direction and securing the bundles with florist pins. Then move on to the outside rim. Do the middle section last and fill in any bare spots. You can add more dried flowers at the end, securing them with a hot glue gun. Hang the wreath where it won't be affected by sun, weather, or heat. If you used fresh herbs, let the wreath lie on a flat surface for several days so none of the herbs droop.

Seasonal Wreath

To create a seasonal wreath, cover a frame with sweet Annie, with another type of artemisia, or with lamb's ears. Then add various herbs and flowers according to the time of year: pink flowers for Valentine's Day, green and silver herbs and red berries (holly or nandina) for Christmas, orange blooms or dried hot peppers for October and November, and so on.

Kitchen Wreath

Cover the wreath form with fresh or dried sage (green or silver leaves), then add bundles of other herbs—purple-leaved basil, dill flowers, rosemary, marjoram, variegated sage, bergamot blooms, parsley, and whole garlic. If you're going to use the herbs for cooking, do it soon, because the wreath will get dusty. You can "dust" herb wreaths with a hair dryer on the lowest setting.

Fragrant Bay Leaf Wreath

Cut fresh bay branches into short sprigs and attach a wooden floral pick to each. Insert the picks into a small straw wreath form, starting from the inside and working in one direction. (If you use a grapevine or wire wreath form, you'll probably have to attach the leaves with a hot glue gun.)

How to Make Herbal Vinegars

Salads suddenly become more interesting when the salad dressing is made with a flavored vinegar. This is an easy project and makes a great gift for foodies. You can experiment with not only a variety of herbs (singly or in combination), but also a number of different kinds of vinegars—cider vinegar, distilled white vinegar, rice wine vinegar, white or red wine vinegar, and so on.

There are numerous methods, all of which work well. Here are two of them. Choose whichever is easiest for you.

Method 1: Place fresh herbs in a clean 1-quart jar. The amount is up to you, but a good guideline in the beginning is to use equal amounts of fresh herbs and vinegar. Pour vinegar over the herbs so that they're completely immersed. Cover the opening with plastic wrap. Set aside for 10 days to 2 weeks in a dark place. To see if it's ready, pull the plastic wrap back and sniff. If you can smell the herbs and not just the vinegar, it's ready. Strain out the herbs and pour the vinegar into nice-looking sterilized bottles. If desired, add a fresh stalk of whatever herb you used to make the vinegar—this will make the bottles look pretty. Top each bottle with a cork or other nonmetal lid. (Metal reacts with the vinegar.)

■ **Method 2:** Place fresh herbs in a saucepan. Cover with the vinegar of your choice. Heat the mixture slightly, but never let it come to a boil. Pour the mixture into a crock or large glass container and cover with a nonmetal lid or plastic wrap. Set aside in a dark place for 5 or 6 days. To see if it's ready, sniff to see if you smell a strong herb odor. If you do, strain out the herbs and pour the vinegar into nice-looking sterilized bottles. Add a stalk of fresh herb, if you like. Seal each bottle with a cork or other nonmetal lid.

Note: Some gardeners don't strain the herbs out of the vinegar before they bottle it. You may want to try one bottle each way, to see which you prefer.

Good Herbs for Vinegar

Basil (especially purple basil, which turns vinegar a pretty pink color)

Borage flowers

Chives (including the flowers, which turn vinegar pink)

Dill

Garlic

Lavender

Marjoram

Mint

Rosemary

Tarragon

Thyme

Enhancing the Flavor

To kick up the flavor a notch, add one or more of these ingredients to a vinegar made with a single herb.

Bay leaves

Hot peppers, dried

Dill seeds

Garlic cloves

Herb Combinations for Vinegar

Basil, garlic, and hot peppers

Rosemary and thyme

Dill and lemon thyme

Rosemary and sage

Basil, rosemary, and winter savory

Chives and garlic

Natural Beauty: Herbal Bath Products and Cosmetics

More and more today, the trend in personal care products is toward natural ingredients. We prefer Mother Nature's fragrances and want to know what's in the products we put on our bodies. Homemade herbal bath products and cosmetics have two more big advantages for those who grow herbs—they're inexpensive and readily available. Here are some to try.

Rosemary Shampoo

2 teaspoons dried rosemary or 1$^1/_2$ tablespoons fresh rosemary

1 cup water

Baby shampoo

Place the rosemary in a heatproof glass bowl. Bring the water to a boil and pour over the rosemary. Cover and let stand overnight. Strain the mixture and mix 1 part herb mixture to 3 parts baby shampoo. Makes about 4 cups of shampoo.

Shiny Hair Rinse

1$^1/_2$ teaspoons dried chamomile, rosemary, or sage

2 cups water

1 tablespoon vinegar

Place the chamomile, rosemary, or sage in a heatproof glass bowl. Bring the water to a boil and pour over the herbs. Cover and let stand until cool. Strain the mixture and mix with vinegar. Use after shampooing. Makes about 2 cups.

Herbal Bath Sachets

Making herbal bath sachets is fun. Depending on your mood and the available herbs, you can create a variety of scents. The simplest method is to place ½ to 1 cup of your favorite dried herb or 1½ to 2 cups of the fresh herb in a bag made of muslin, cheesecloth, or old clean pantyhose. When you run the bath, hold the bag under the hot water faucet, and then float the bag in the bath. Discard fresh herbs afterward. If you like, you can let a bag of dried herbs dry out and use it once more.

Another method is to create a "bath tea" to add to the tub. Place 1 cup of dried herbs or 2 cups of fresh herbs in a pan and cover with water. Bring to a boil, cover, and let stand for 15 minutes. Strain the "tea" into the bath as the tub is filling with water. (You can avoid the straining if you place the herbs in sachets instead of placing them directly in the pan.)

Good Herbs for Baths

Chamomile flowers

Lavender flowers

Lemon balm

Lemongrass

Marjoram

Mint

Thyme

Rose petals

Lavender Bath Salts

4 cups kosher salt

1 cup dried lavender

Mix together the salt and lavender and store in a pretty container beside the tub. To use, spoon the mixture into a spice sachet or tea ball and place under the running faucet. Alternatively, package the salts in small cloth sachets to avoid having the lavender loose in the water. You can use sea salt in place of kosher salt, but it's expensive. Yield: about 5 cups.

Peppermint Facial Sauna

Place 2 tablespoons dried peppermint (or $1/2$ cup fresh) in a large saucepan and add 8 cups water. Bring to a boil, remove from the heat, and place on a trivet. Hold your face over the steam (using a thick towel to direct the steam) for 10 to 15 minutes. Then splash your face with cold water, dry, and apply a moisturizer.

Easiest Herbs to Grow

Artemisia (southernwood)
Basil
Bergamot
Borage
Chives
Cilantro/Coriander
Dill
Fennel
Lemon balm
Mint
Oregano
Rue

Herbs Nutrition Chart

Many people are surprised to find that culinary herbs can be powerhouses of nutrition. Here's a sampling of the nutritional values of some of the herbs mentioned in this book.

Herb	Nutrition
Anise (seeds)	Iron, calcium, Vitamin C, manganese, and potassium
Anise hyssop	Vitamin C, calcium, iron
Basil	Vitamin K, iron, calcium, Vitamin A, Vitamin C, dietary fiber, manganese, and potassium
Bay	Iron, Vitamin A, Vitamin C, Vitamin B6, manganese, calcium, and dietary fiber
Borage	Vitamin A, Vitamin C, iron, calcium, magnesium, potassium, manganese
Caraway	Dietary fiber, magnesium, potassium, Vitamin C, protein
Chervil	Iron, potassium, calcium, Vitamin A
Chives	Vitamin A, Vitamin C, iron, Vitamin K
Cilantro/Coriander	Vitamin C, iron, calcium, Vitamin A, potassium, Vitamin K, (seeds—dietary fiber)
Dill	Vitamin A, Vitamin C, iron, potassium, calcium
Fennel	Dietary fiber, calcium, Vitamin C, iron, protein
Garlic	Vitamin C, calcium, iron, dietary fiber, Vitamin B6
Horseradish	Vitamin C, dietary fiber, calcium, potassium
Lemon grass	Iron, magnesium, manganese, potassium
Marjoram	Iron, calcium, Vitamin A, Vitamin K, Vitamin C, manganese, dietary fiber

Herb	Nutrition
Oregano	Iron, calcium, Vitamin A, Vitamin K, Vitamin C, dietary fiber, manganese
Parsley	Iron, Vitamin A, Vitamin C, Vitamin K, calcium, potassium
Peppermint	Vitamin A, Vitamin C, manganese
Rosemary	Iron, calcium, Vitamin C, Vitamin B6, magnesium, Vitamin A
Sage	Iron, calcium, magnesium, Vitamin B6, Vitamin A, dietary fiber
Savory	Calcium, iron, Vitamin A, Vitamin B6, Vitamin C, manganese, magnesium
Sorrel	Vitamin A, Vitamin C
Spearmint	Vitamin A, iron, dietary fiber, Vitamin C, manganese, calcium
Tarragon	Iron, calcium, Vitamin B6, Vitamin C, Vitamin A, potassium, protein, magnesium
Thyme	Iron, calcium, Vitamin A, Vitamin C, magnesium

Note: Dried and fresh herbs may have different nutritional values. For more complete information, visit the USDA National Nutrient Database at http://www.nal.usda.gov/fnic/foodcomp/search.

Sources of Herb Seeds and Plants

W. Atlee Burpee Co.
300 Park Avenue
Warminster, PA 18924
(800) 333-5808
www.burpee.com

The Cook's Garden
300 Park Avenue
Warminster, PA 18924
(800) 457-9703
www.cooksgarden.com

Goodwin Creek Gardens
P.O. Box 83
Williams, OR 97544
(800) 846-7359
www.goodwincreekgardens.com

Johnny's Selected Seeds
955 Benton Avenue
Winslow, ME 04901
(877) 564-6697
www.johnnyseeds.com

Nichols Garden Nursery
1190 Old Salem Road NE
Albany, OR 97321
(800) 422-3985
www.nicholsgardennursery.com

Renee's Garden
6060A Graham Hill Road
Felton, CA 95018
(888) 880-7228
www.reneesgarden.com

Richters Herbs
357 Highway 47
Goodwood, ON L0C 1A0
Canada
(800) 668-4372
www.richters.com

Seeds of Change
P.O. Box 15700
Santa Fe, NM, 87506
(888) 800-762-7333
www.seedsofchange.com

Well-Sweep Herb Farm
205 Mt. Bethel Road
Port Murray, NJ 07865
(908) 852-5390
www.wellsweep.com

Bibliography

Chase, Nan K. *Eat Your Yard.* Layton, UT: Gibbs Smith, 2010

Gardner, Jo Ann. *Herbs in Bloom.* Portland, OR: Timber Press, 1998

Hanson, Beth, editor. *Fragrant Designs.* Brooklyn, NY: Brooklyn Botanic Garden, 2009

Hepper, F. Nigel. *Planting a Bible Garden.* Grand Rapids, MI: Fleming H. Revell, 1997

Hill, Madalene and Barclay, Gwen. *Southern Herb Growing.* Fredericksburg, TX: Shearer Publishing, 1987

Loewer, Peter. *The Evening Garden.* Portland, OR: Timber Press, 2002

McClure, Susan. *The Herb Gardener.* Pownal, VT: Garden Way Publishing, 1996

McVicar, Jekka. *The Complete Herb Book.* Buffalo, NY: Firefly Books, 2008

Moldenke, Harold N. and Moldenke, Alma L. *Plants of the Bible.* New York: Dover Publications, 1952

Musselman, Lytton John. *Figs, Dates, Laurel, and Myrrh.* Portland, OR: Timber Press, 2007

Platt, Ellen Spector. *Lavender.* Mechanicsburg, PA: Stackpole Books, 2009

Oster, Maggie. *All About Herbs.* Des Moines, IA: Meredith Books, 1999

Swenson, Allan A. *Herbs of the Bible.* New York: Kensington Publishing, 2003

Scoble, Gretchen and Field, Ann. *The Meaning of Herbs.* San Francisco: Chronicle Books, 2001

Trail, Gayla. *Grow Great Grub.* New York: Clarkson Potter, 2010

Turcotte, Patricia. *The New England Herb Gardener.* Woodstock, VT: Countryman Press, 1990

Wilson, Jim. *Landscaping With Herbs.* Boston: Houghton Mifflin Co., 1994

Photo & Illustration Credits

Elayne Sears (all illustrations are by Elayne Sears unless otherwise noted)
Pages: Front cover illustration, 6, 22, 24 (top illustration), 28, 30, 34, 38, 40, 43, 46, 51, 54, 60, 63, 68, 72, 74, 77, 80, 83, 86, 90, 92, 98, 102, 170

Thinkstock
Pages: 6, 10, 11, 12, 14, 15, 16, 18, 20, 24 (bottom illustration), 27, 31, 32, 33, 39, 42, 45, 48, 50, 53, 56, 57, 64, 65, 66, 70, 71, 76, 78, 79, 82, 84 (illustration), 88, 91, 94, 96, 97 (illustration), 100, 158, 159, 160, 161 (illustration), 162, 165, 166, 167, 168, 169, 172, 173, 174 (illustration), 177

Tom Eltzroth
Pages: 106, 107, 108, 117, 119, 120, 122, 123, 126, 128, 129, 130, 131, 132, 138, 139, 143, 144, 145, 148, 151, 156

iStockphoto
Pages: Back cover, 36, 110, 113, 114, 115, 116, 118, 125, 134, 135, 137, 140, 150, 153, 154

Jerry Pavia
Pages: 133, 142, 147, 152, 157

National Garden Bureau
Pages: 58, 59

Liz Ball
Page: 121

Roz Creasy
Page: 149

Cindy Games
Page: 95

Monrovia
Page: 109

NPS Photo (from Wind Cave National Park)
Page: 127

Andre Viette
Page: 112

A book for any gardener, anywhere.

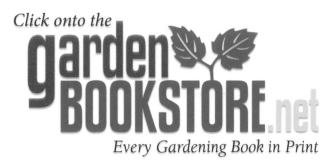

Meet Judy

Judy Lowe has had a lifelong love of gardening, and has been writing about it for more than twenty-five years. She became interested in gardening through her mother, who could grow *anything*. Although Lowe had no idea that she could use horticulture knowledge professionally, her early background compelled her to take horticulture classes in college, while majoring in English. Thus was born a garden writer.

Lowe has been the garden editor of the *Chattanooga Times-Free Press* in Chattanooga, Tennessee and *The Christian Science Monitor* in Boston, Massachusetts. She has been active in the Garden Writers Association (a group consisting of more than 2,000 members), serving on the board for fourteen years and as president for two years.

Lowe's ten previous books include these for Cool Springs Press, *Tennessee & Kentucky Gardener's Guide* and *Month-by-Month*

Gardening in Tennessee and Kentucky, and *Ortho's All About Pruning*. Her numerous articles have appeared in many magazines, including *Woman's Day* and *Southern Living*. Her work has won awards from the Garden Writers Association, the National Garden Bureau, and many other groups.

Judy and her husband have lived—and gardened—in a number of places in the United States (and overseas). This has given her wide personal experience in growing herbs and other plants in many different soils and climates. They currently live in South Carolina, but no matter where Lowe lives, helping gardeners is her life's goal.